Political Trends

REVIVAL OF TWO PARTY SYSTEM IN INDIA

Ruling vs. Combined Opposition

Political Trends
REVIVAL OF TWO PARTY SYSTEM IN INDIA
Ruling vs. Combined Opposition

By
Dr. Janak Raj Jai
Rajiv Jai

Regency Publications
New Delhi

ISBN 81-86030-16-6

Published by Regency Publications, 20/36-G, Old Market, West Patel Nagar, New Delhi 110 008, and printed at Radiant Printers, New Delhi 110 008, Phones: 571 2539, 574 0038; Telefax: 578 3571.

"The leaders are men of clay, they are not saints or fakirs; the people are the masters and these leaders are the servants, the public must be vigilant and keep a constant eye on the style of functioning of the Government"

Acharya Kriplani

Dedicated to the
Fourth Estate which
highlighted the political events
without fear or favour

The co-author Rajiv Jai with Smt. Sonia Gandhi

PREFACE

India is one of the largest democracies of the world. So long as there was single largest party rule without crutches at the centre, things went very well. But unfortunately, after the coalition governments came into being, continuity of policies, uninterrupted progress, and stability went on a long holiday. Almost all the institutions started denigrating; peace, prosperity, and law and order became one of the biggest casualties. Need for outside support to survive has become a cause of exploitation by quite a few allies.

Prime Minister Atal Behari Vajpayee has himself admitted that the democracy in India has become hollow and the "politics is becoming increasingly criminalised." Wondering whether democratic institutions were discharging their responsibilities properly, and whether democracy had taken deep roots in the country, he said, "while searching for answers to the question, one is sorely disappointed."

With the active participation of Smt. Sonia Gandhi as the head of the Congress Party, a new ray of hope has indeed appeared in the positive direction on the national political scene. We have discussed all these aspects in the present book, and have earnestly made out a case in favour of single largest party rule, with strong, constructive, and healthy opposition. We have also traced out the political history of our country, right from Jawaharlal Nehru to Atal Behari Vajpayee. The recent Assembly elections in four states was nothing but a contest between Sonia Gandhi and Atal Behari Vajpayee, and as such was a mini referendum on the performance of the BJP Government. The helplessness and haplessness of Prime Minister Atal Behari Vajpayee at the hands of his allies, as also the differences between him and the President of BJP,

Kushabhau Thakre, surfaced in a big way at the Bangalore Meet, have also been highlighted in the present work. Sushma's night rounds at the police stations, her alleged bunglings and messing-up in the onion deal, and her alleged connections with Romesh Sharma form part of this book.

Kudos to the media for their bold, and upright exposures of the political events without fear or favour. We in fact have dedicated this book to the Fourth Estate, without whose help the vital problems facing the country could not have been focussed in right perspective.

We sincerely hope that the voters, who are the real masters, shall always give a clear mandate in favour of single-party-rule, to keep the democracy in good health.

Avtar Singh Sohal, a dear colleague, has enriched this book by contributing an interesting, informative and indepth article 'Akali Antics.' Krishan Gopal Sharma, and Inayat-Ullah, my old fellow colleagues, have always been a source of inspiration.

My son Rajiv, deserves every appreciation for sharing equal burden in the accomplishment of this task. My wife, Santosh, is always with me as a true life partner.

C-50, Rajpur Khurd Colony,
Sewa Sadan,
New Delhi 110 068
February, 1999

Dr. Janak Raj Jai
L II/68, Lajpat Nagar,
New Delhi 110 024
Ph. 6932057, 6803 447

INDIA 1998 AT A GLANCE

January 15: Veteran Freedom Fighter and former Prime Minister Gulzari Lal Nanda, 100, dies in Ahmedabad.

February 21: Governor Romesh Bhandari dismisses Kalyan Singh government in Uttar Pradesh and installed Jagdambika Prasad a new Chief Minister.

February 23: Kalyan Singh reinstated by a landmark judgment delivered by the High Court.

Mulayam Laloo float a new front—Rashtriya Lok Tantrick Morcha—attempting to build a "Third Alternative."

March 12: BJP emerges as largest party in 12th general elections to the Lok Sabha; forms coalition government with the help of 18 allies. Atal Behari Vajpayee takes over as the first BJP Prime Minister of Indian Republic.

March 14: Sonia Gandhi enters active politics; takes over as President of Indian National Congress removing Sita Ram Kesri with the exercise of special power by the Congress Working Committee.

March 19: CPM veteran leader E.M.S. Namboodripad dies in Thiruvananthapuram.

April 14: Kushabhau Thakre was elected as the President of the Bharatiya Janata Party.

May 11: India conducts three nuclear tests in Pokhran range in Rajasthan followed by two more on May 13.

May 12: Prime Minister declares India a Nuclear State.

Pakistan follows with similar tests later in the month.

August 6: Shiv Sena supremo Bal Thackeray indicted by Srikrishna Report on 1992 Mumbai riots; The Maharashtra State Government rejects the said report.

August 15: Year long celebrations for fifty years of independence comes to an end; Prime Minister delivers his speech from the Red Fort.

Bharat Ratna for M. Subha Lakshmi, C. Subramaniam and Lok Nayak Jayaprakash Narayan.

Dropsy claims over 50 lives on account of contaminated mustard oil.

August 18: VDIS nets a bonanza of Rs. 10,050 crores; Rs. 33,000 black money comes out.

September 25: President K.R. Narayanan rejects government's recommendation of Central rule in Bihar.

October 13: Controversy erupts over the film 'FIRE', following Shiv Sena protests.

October 21: Alleged Dawood Frontman and property grabber Romesh Sharma arrested in Delhi.

November 19: Six-member National Security Council formed.

November 25–30: Congress wins Assembly elections in Madhya Pradesh, Rajasthan and Delhi.

Sushma Swaraj humbled—resigns her Assembly seat, and retains the Parliament seat. Swears by Gita denying any link whatsoever with Romesh Sharma.

CONTENTS

MODEL CODE OF CONDUCT

The Constitution of India has devised certain independent authorities to deal with particular matters. These are:

1) Comptroller and Auditor General of India,
2) Election Commission of India; and
3) Union Public Service Commission.

Election Commission of India: Article 324 of the Constitution of India prescribes that superintendence, direction and control of election shall be vested in the Election Commission of India.

The Election Commission of India has to look after a variety of administrative matters and practical problems, as also to maintain contact with the administrative authorities of the Centre as well as in the States of the country. The Election Commission has also to perform quasi-judicial function. The Commission has also the responsibility of overseeing the entire electoral process. In order to ensure uniformity of electoral procedure and practice in all the units, and for the greatest safeguard for the purity of election, it was decided that there should be an All India Election Commission with jurisdiction over both Union and State elections.

To perform this onerous task, the Election Commission of India has prescribed the Model Code of Conduct which has to be adhered to by all the candidates, and the political parties, applicable for the Lok Sabha as well as Assembly elections throughout the country.

The latest Model Code of Conduct for the guidance of political parties and candidates is reproduced as follows.

I. General Conduct

(1) No party or candidate shall indulge in any activity which may aggravate existing differences or create mutual hatred or cause tension between different castes and communities, religious or linguistic.

(2) Criticism of other political parties, when made, shall be confined to their policies and programme, past record and work. Parties and candidates shall refrain from criticism of all respects of private life, not connected with the public activities of the leaders or workers of other parties. Criticism of other parties or their workers based on unverified allegations or on distortion shall be avoided.

(3) There shall be no appeal to caste or communal feelings for securing votes. Mosques, churches, temples or other places of worship shall not be used as forum for election propaganda.

(4) All parties and candidates shall avoid scrupulously all activities which are 'corrupt practices' and offences under the election law, such as bribing of voters, intimidation of voters, impersonation of voters, canvassing within 100 meters of polling station, holding public meetings during the period of 48 hours ending with the hour fixed for the close of the poll, and the transport and conveyance of voters to and from polling station.

5. The right of every individual for peaceful and undisturbed home life shall be respected, however, much the political parties or candidates, may resent his political opinions or activities. Organising demonstrations or picketing before the houses of individuals by way of protesting against their opinions or activities shall not be resorted to under any circumstances.

6. No political party or candidate shall permit its or his followers to make use of any individual's land, building, compound wall etc., without his permission, for erecting flag staffs, suspending banners, pasting notices, writing slogans etc.

7. Political parties and candidates shall ensure that their supporters do not create obstructions in or breakup meetings and processions organised by other parties. Workers or

sympathisers of one political party shall not create disturbances at public meetings organised by another political party by putting questions orally or in writing or by distributing leaflets of their own party. Processions shall not be taken out by a party along places at which meetings are being held by another party. Posters issued by any party shall not be removed by workers of another party.

II. Meetings.

1. The party or candidate shall inform the local police authorities of the venue and time of any proposed meeting well in time so as to enable the police to make necessary arrangements for controlling traffic and maintaining peace and order.
2. A party or candidate shall ascertain in advance if there are any restrictive or prohibitory orders in force in the place proposed for the meeting. If such orders exist, they shall be followed strictly. If any exemption is required from such orders, it shall be applied for and obtained well in time.
3. If permission or licence is to be obtained for the use of loudspeakers or any other facility in connection with any proposed meeting, the party or candidate shall apply to the authority concerned well in advance and obtain such permission or licence.
4. Organisers of a meeting shall invariably seek the assistance of police on duty for dealing with persons disturbing a meeting or otherwise attempting to create disorder. Organisers themselves shall not take action against such persons.

III. Processions

1. A party or candidate organising a procession shall decide before hand, the time and place of starting of the procession, the route to be followed, and the time and place at which the procession will terminate. There shall ordinarily be no deviation from the programme.

2. The organisers shall give advance intimation to the local police authorities of the programme so as to enable the later to make necessary arrangements.
3. The organisers shall ascertain if any restrictive orders are in force in the localities through which the procession has to pass, and shall comply with the restrictions unless exempted specially by competent authority. Any traffic regulations or restrictions shall also be carefully adhered to.
4. The organisers shall take steps in advance to arrange for passage of the procession so that there is no block or hindrance to traffic. If the procession is very long, it shall be organised in segments of suitable lengths, so that at convenient intervals, especially at points where the procession has to pass road junctions, the passage of held up traffic could be allowed by stages thus avoiding heavy traffic congestion.
5. Processions shall be regulated as to keep as much to the right of the road as possible and the direction and advice of the police on duty shall be strictly complied with.
6. If two or more political parties or candidates propose to take processions over the same route or parts thereof at about the same time, the organisers shall establish contact well in advance and decide upon the measures to be taken to see that the processions do not clash or cause hindrance to traffic. The assistance of the local police shall be availed of for arriving at a satisfactory arrangement. For this purpose the parties shall contact the police at the earliest opportunity.
7. The political parties or candidates shall exercise control to the maximum extent possible in the matter of processionists carrying articles which may be put to misuse by undesirable elements especially in moments of excitement.
8. The carrying of effigies purporting to represent members of other political parties or their leaders, burning such effigies in public and such other forms of demonstration shall not be countenanced by any political party or candidate.

IV. Polling Day

All political parties and candidates shall,

(i) cooperate with the officers on election duty to ensure peaceful and orderly polling and complete freedom to the voters to exercise their franchise without being subjected to any annoyance, or obstruction;

(ii) supply to their authorised workers suitable badges or identity cards;

(iii) agree that the identity slips supplied by them to voters shall be on plain (white) paper and shall not contain any symbol, name of the candidate or the name of the party;

(iv) refrain from serving or distributing liquor on polling day; and during the twenty-four hours preceding it;

(v) not allow unnecessary crowd to be collected near the camps set up by the political parties and candidates near the polling booths so as to avoid confrontation and tension among workers and sympathisers of the parties and candidate;

(vi) ensure that the candidate's camp shall be simple. They shall not display any posters, flags, symbols or any other propaganda material. No eatables shall be served; no crowd allowed in the camps; and

(vii) cooperate with the authorities in complying with the restrictions to be imposed on the plying of vehicles on the polling day and obtain permits for them which should be displayed prominently on those vehicles.

V. Polling Booth

Excepting the voters, no one without a valid pass from the Election Commission shall enter the polling booths.

VI. Observers

The Election Commission is appointing observers. If the candidates or their agents have any specific complaint or problem regarding the conduct of the elections they may bring the same to the notice of the observer.

VII. Party in Power

The party in power whether at the Centre or in the State or states concerned shall ensure that no cause is given for any complaint that it has used its official position for the purposes of its election campaign, and in particular—

(i) (a) The ministers shall not combine their official visit with electioneering work and shall not also make use of official machinery or personnel during electioneering work;

(b) The government transport including official aircrafts, vehicles, machinery and personnel shall not be used for furtherance of the interest of the party in power.

(ii) Public places such as maidans etc., for holding election meetings and use of helipads for airflights in connection with elections, shall not be monopolised by itself. Other parties and candidates shall be allowed the use of such places and facilities on the same terms and conditions on which they are used by the party in power;

(iii) Rest houses, dak bungalows or other government accommodation shall not be monopolised by the party in power to its candidates and such accommodation shall be allowed to be used by other parties and candidates in a fair manner but no party or candidate shall use or be allowed to use such accommodation (including premises appertaining thereto) as a campaign office or for holding any public meeting for the purposes of election propaganda;

(iv) Issue of advertisement at the cost of public exchequer in the newspapers and other media and the misuse of official mass media during the election period for partisan coverage of political news and publicity regarding achievements, with a view to furthering the prospects of the party in power shall be scrupulously avoided;

(v) Ministers and other authorities shall not sanction grants/payments out of discretionary funds from the time elections are announced by the commission; and

(vi) From the time the elections are announced by the commission, Ministers and other authorities shall not—

(a) announce any financial grants in any form or premises thereof; or

(b) lay foundation stones etc., of projects or schemes of any kind; or

(c) make any promise of construction of roads, provision of drinking water facilities etc.,

(d) make any adhoc appointments in government, public undertakings etc.

which may have the effect of influencing the voters in favour of the party in power.

(vii) Ministers of Central or State Government shall not enter any polling station or place of counting except in their capacity as a candidate or voter or authorised agent.

THE NATIONAL POLITICAL SCENE

Jawaharlal Nehru to Indira Gandhi

The history of the Indian National Congress is the history of the independence movement. During the course of its long history the Congress identified itself with the political life of the people and it has emerged as the greatest single instrument of political unity and social change.

The Indian National Congress, under the leadership of Mahatma Gandhi, always held the view that freedom could not mean merely the termination of an alien rule. It could have real significance only if it meant the ending of exploitation, eradication of poverty and the establishment of a free and egalitarian society.

In free India Jawaharlal Nehru made a successful effort to reconcile the practice of democracy with the pursuit of socialism. In 1955, at Avadi (Madras now Tamil Nadu), the Indian National Congress officially declared as its goal the establishment of a socialistic pattern of society. India's struggle, therefore, has been essentially for freedom from want of hunger, from poverty and squalor, from exploitation and discrimination.

The Congress Party headed by Pandit Jawaharlal Nehru indeed ruled the country until he died in the year 1964. He, in fact, continued to be the darling of the people so long as he lived and remained as the Prime Minister of India. After his death on 27th May, 1964, Shri Lal Bahadur Shastri became the next Prime Minister. Because of his mysterious death, in Russia, he could rule the country as its Prime Minister for 18 months only. Then started the era of Shrimati Indira Gandhi from 1966 onwards, until she was defeated in the year 1977, because of the excesses committed during emergency.

In the first Lok Sabha election in 1952, the Congress secured 364 seats out of a total 489. In the second in 1957, the Congress won 371 seats out of 494. And in the year 1962, the Congress party secured 361 seats out of 494. After the death of Jawaharlal Nehru, the Congress in the year 1967, secured 283 seats out of 520, but in 1971, the Congress bagged 352 seats out of 518. The continuous return of the Congress to power had certainly helped the country maintain continuity in policy and uninterrupted progress.

After 1971, the next elections to the Lok Sabha, were held in the year 1977, as the life of the Parliament was extended. During the year 1975, Shrimati Indira Gandhi declared emergency and lakhs of people belonging to the opposition political parties were sent to Jail. Censorship was imposed and the people were deprived of their fundamental rights. This act of Mrs. Indira Gandhi certainly made her unpopular. Jaya Prakash Narayan then gave a call for total revolution, and as such all the opposition political parties responded to the call of JP and fought elections under his leadership. The result was obvious, the people rejected Indira Gandhi and for the first time in the post independent history of India, a non Congress government came into power, giving a crushing defeat to the Congress Party. But the Janata Party which came into power in 1977, could not complete its full term, because of infighting by the leaders belonging to different ghataks. The people again pinned their hopes in the Congress Party and brought back Indira Gandhi as the next Prime Minister of India on 14th January, 1980.

Here is the diary of events right from 26th January, 1950 (when the Constitution came into force) until the 14th January, 1980 when Indira Gandhi again emerged as the Prime Minister of India.

Diary of Events

1950
January 26: The Constitution comes into force.

1951

December 10: Polling begins for the First Lok Sabha Election (ended on 21.2.52).

1952

May 11: The first session of the Lok Sabha under the Constitution held (at 10.45 A.M.).

May 13: The new Cabinet, after India's first general Election, sworn in.

1957

February 24: Polling begins for the second Lok Sabha election (ended 14.3.57).

April 5: India's first Communist Government takes office in Kerala.

1962

February 16–27: Polling held for the Third Lok Sabha Election.

1964

May 27: Jawaharlal Nehru dies.

1967

February 15–22: Polling for the fourth Lok Sabha Election held.

1969

November 22: Congress Party splits into two.

December 17: Congress (O) accorded formal recognition as an opposition party in Parliament. (This had happened for the first time in the hisotry of the Indian Parliament because no single opposition party had till then commanded the required number of seats in the Lok Sabha).

1970

December 27: The fourth Lok Sabha dissolved.

1971

March 1–10: Polling for the fifth Lok Sabha held (mid term poll).

March 14: The ruling Congress Party achieves massive victory at the polls, capturing two-third of the Lok Sabha seats.

1974

August 29: Bharatiya Lok Dal (BLD) launches as a new party, merging seven opposition parties which include BKD, SSP and Swatantra Party, but exclude Congress (O) and Jana Sangh.

1975

June 12: The Allahabad High Court sets aside Mrs. Gandhi's election to the Lok Sabha from the Rae Bareily constituency.

June 9–11: Gujarat elections held (on 12.6.75, opposition united front emerges victorious and forms the government).

June 24: The Supreme court vacation Judge Justice V.R. Krishna Iyer grants to Mrs. Gandhi a partial stay of the Allahabad High Court Judgement of 12.6.75.

June 25: A state of internal emergency proclaimed in India. Mass arrests of opposition leaders take place. Press censorship imposed.

November 7: The Supreme Court upholds Mrs. Gandhi's election to the Lok Sabha and sets aside the Allahabad High Court judgement of 12.6.75. The Supreme court at the same time strikes down a provision in the Constitution (Thirty ninth amendment) Act for violating the Constitution's basic structure. (The provision struck down said that notwithstanding any order made by any court declaring an election as void, such election shall continue to be valid and that any such order and any such findings of a court shall be deemed to have been void).

1976

February 4: The Lok Sabha's life extended by one year.

November 5: The Lok Sabha votes to extend its own life by another year.

1977

January 19: Lok Sabha dissolved and fresh elections (mid term poll) ordered to be held in March, 1977. (Mrs. Gandhi had made an announcement the previous day.)

January 23: Janata Party formed, composed of Congress(O), Jana Sangh, BLD, and SSP with Morarji Desai as Chairman.

February 2: Jagjivan Ram resigns from the Central Cabinet and the Congress Party. Forms a new party Congress for Democracy.

March 16–18, 19, 20: Polling held for the sixth Lok Sabha.

March 19: Polling held for the sixth Kerala Assembly Elections (The ruling United Front emerged victorious).

March 21–23: The ruling Congress Party routed in the elections. The Janata Party secured an absolute majority.

March 23: The Morarji Desai Government takes office.

March 26: Neelam Sanjiva Reddy (Janata Party) unanimously elected Speaker of the sixth Lok Sabha. (Ram Niwas Mirdha, (Congress) unanimously elected Deputy Chairman of the Rajya Sabha on 30.3.77).

April 5: For the first time since independence an opposition party is invited to broadcast to the nation from All India Radio. (Prime Minister Morarji Desai broadcast on April 4, and the leader of the Congress Opposition Party in Parliament, Y.B. Chavan, on April 5.)

April 9: Assemblies of nine States dissolved.

April 30: Presidential proclamation issued under Article 356 of the Constitution for Central rule in the nine Congress ruled States—Punjab, Haryana, Himachal Pradesh, Bihar, Rajasthan, Orissa, Madhya Pradesh, Uttar Pradesh and West Bengal.

June 1: Polling held for the Goa, Daman and Diu Assembly (The ruling Maharashtrawadi Gomantak Party emerges victorious for the fourth time in succession, and forms the new Government on June 7).

June 10–14: Polling held for assemblies in ten States and Councils in two Union Territories.

1978

January 2: The Congress party splits a second time. Mrs. Gandhi's party thereafter came to be known as Congress(I).

February 25: Andhra Pradesh, Assam, Karnataka, Maharashtra, Meghalaya and Arunachal Pradesh go to the polls.

June 29: Charan Singh is asked to resign from Cabinet.

November 8: Mrs. Gandhi declared elected as a member of Parliament from Chikmagalur in Karnataka, defeating Virendra Patil by a margin of over 77,000 votes.

December 19: The Lok Sabha passes a resolution sentencing Mrs. Indira Gnadhi to imprisonment till the end of its winter session, and expelling her from the House on a charge of breach of privilege (Mrs. Gandhi was arrested soon after the passage of resolution and kept in Tihar Jail for a week).

1979

January 24: Charan Singh rejoins the Central Cabinet as Deputy Prime Minister and Finance Minister. Jagjivan Ram also becomes Deputy PM.

March 9: The Lok Sabha passes the official Special Courts Bill. (The Rajya Sabha passed it on 21.3.79 with two major amendments).

June 24: Devraj Urs expelled from Congress(I) for six years.

June 29: Charan Singh and Raj Narain resign from the Central Cabinet.

July 15: Morarji Desai submits resignation of his cabinet.

July 18: The President invites Y.B. Chavan to explore possibilities of forming a new Government.

July 22: Chavan reports failure to President.

July 23: The President asks Morarji Desai and Charan Singh to submit lists of supporters.

July 26: The President invites Charan Singh to form a new Government.

1980

January 3, 6: India goes to the polls to elect the seventh Lok Sabha.

January 14: Mrs. Indira Gandhi sworn in as Prime Minister.

Indira Gandhi to Sonia Gandhi

The fall of Janata Party came 28 months after they came into power. The reason was obvious—infighting among the leaders belonging to different ghataks, and one point programme of the government to punish and humiliate Indira Gandhi in one way or the other. Shah Commission under the chairmanship of Justice J.C. Shah was appointed to go into the excesses committed during emergency. The government media, including the All India Radio went on highlighting the proceedings of the Shah Commission, and a full fledged hate campaign had started against Indira Gandhi.

The people got disappointed as they had high hopes that the Janata Government would work for the welfare of the people. Their genuine hopes and aspirations were thus shattered to pieces. There was complete confusion and disillusionment among the people, as they felt that the Janata Government headed by Morarji Desai was busy in settling personal scores with Indira Gandhi instead of looking into the burning problems of the country as well as the people.

Differences among the leaders reached to such an extent that Morarji Desai had to tender his resignation. Due to lust of power, Charan Singh allowed himself to be trapped, and accepted premiership on the assurance of outside support by Indira Gandhi. Before facing the Parliament, he also fell like pack of cards. The country was thus again pushed into fresh Lok Sabha elections.

The 1980 Lok Sabha elections brought back Indira Gandhi into power, and she stood fully atoned for emergency excesses. It goes without saying that it was the leadership which failed the democratic process, and not the voters who always tried to give the mandate as per the circumstances demanded. Kudos to the Indian voters. They have always tried to vote against the bigger evil.

Rajiv Gandhi Takes an Oath of Office as Prime Minister

The result was that the Congress Party once again came into power under the leadership of Shrimati Indira Gandhi after the 1980 Lok Sabha Elections. But the tragic end of Indira Gandhi's regime came in 1984, when she was brutally assassinated at the hands of her own security guard. After the untimely and unfortunate death of Indira Gandhi, her elder son, Rajiv Gandhi was given an oath of office of the Prime Minister.

Rajiv Gandhi, of course, started his innings with a very good image; he was being called by every one 'Mr. Clean'. But later on he was not able to maintain this image of 'Mr. Clean', may be due to the ill-advice of the coterie around him. He was also involved in the Bofors Controversy on account of which V.P. Singh had to part company, and formed 'Jan Morcha' after having been expelled from the Congress.

Due to the Bofors Controversy Rajiv Gandhi was pressurised to tender resignation. As many as 106 members of Parliament resigned in protest.

Lok Sabha Dissolved

Ultimately the Lok Sabha was dissolved prematurely, in spite of the fact that the ruling party had a massive mandate. After the dastardly murder of Indira Gandhi on 31st October 1984, Rajiv Gandhi remained in power until 1st December 1989. The term of Lok Sabha was to expire on 14th January 1990, but the general elections were held on 22, 24 and 26th November, 1989 because of the dissolution of Parliament prematurely.

Violence during Elections

As we have mentioned above, the general elections to the Lok Sabha were held in the last week of November 1989. During the elections the Bofors issue was highlighted by all the non-Congress parties. The election scene in 1989 was unfortunately marked by widespread violence. There were hundreds of poll clashes and indiscriminate use of lathis, guns, daggers, and bombs. Even in violation of the model code of conduct and the instructions issued by the Election Commission, most of the political parties had shown scant regard for the recommendations and guidelines of the Commission. Almost all the political parties did field some candidates who had criminal record. It included one candidate who had five criminal cases pending against him; another candidate who had been named in more than 30 murder cases, still another candidate who had been detained for organising a bomb attack, and a fourth one charged by the CBI of swindling cooperative funds.

V.P. Singh as Prime Minister

All the anti-Congress parties joined together, and defeated the Congress(I) in the 1989 elections. The political parties with different ideologies, i.e. BJP, CPI, CPI(M) came together and supported the government headed by the National Front, with

Vishwanath Pratap Singh as the Prime Minister. From day one, after V.P. Singh took over as the Prime Minister, he had been facing difficulties after difficulties from different constituents. Chandra Shekhar from the very beginning declared that he did not recognise V.P. Singh as his leader. Choudhry Devi Lal would threaten him, that it was he who made him the Prime Minister. BJP had agreed to extend only issue based support. Therefore, most of the time of V.P. Singh was spent in cajoling and arranging the tables of different constituents. So nothing useful worth the name could be done for the welfare of the people, who had pinned every hope on the National Front.

Mandal Commission

When V.P. Singh sensed that his grip was becoming loose day by day, he dug out the Mandal Commission Report gathering dust on the shelves. To keep himself in perpetual power, he declared that he would implement the Mandal Report in letter and spirit. In fact, this was the gimmic which he tried to play, to gather support from the particular set of vote Banks. There was a great reaction to this declaration. The student community came on the streets in protest against the implementation of the Mandal Report. There were spate of suicide bids, the police lathi charged the students, and lot of blood was seen on the roads. But madness for power did not have any effect on the bad designs of V.P. Singh. He did not even feel sorry for the bloodshed caused by this declaration, inspite of strong resistance from many quarters.

BJP's Rath Yatra

In reply to the declaration of the implementation of the Mandal Report the BJP came out with a counter attack and raised the Ayodhya issue, to gain sympathy and attract the particular strata of society. Atal Bihari Vajpayee is on record to say, "*Tumne Mandal Kiya, To Hamne Kamandal Kiya.*"

Thus this was the beginning of the era of the caste and class war. People belonging to different schools of thought got very much disgusted, as they felt cheated by the National

Front Government. Lal Krishna Advani took out 'Rath Yatra' to reach Ayodhya, but as soon the rath entered Bihar, he was arrested by Laloo Prasad Yadav, the then Chief Minister. At that point of time, the BJP had no other alternative than to withdraw its support from the government headed by V.P. Singh. And that was the end of the marriage between the BJP and the National Front.

Author Meets V.P. Singh

After this incident, naturally the National Front Government came to an end. The author had the opportunity to be very close to V.P. Singh. The author and his two very senior colleagues— Krishan Gopal Sharma and Inayat Ullah went to the official residence of V.P. Singh. We had a very cordial talk with the Raja. Rani Sahiba was gracious enough to entertain us personally with a cup of tea. But even this hospitability did not reduce our pain and agony. We closed the door and had heart to heart talk. The Raja listened to us with great patience, and did not utter a word. Before we parted, Krishan Gopal Sharma, a senior colleague abruptly said,

"Raja Sahib, you have betrayed yourself,
You have betrayed the country
and
You have betrayed your friends."

He further said, "Please do ponder over what we have uttered, before you go to bed tonight."

We must say that the Raja took all this in a spirit in which we expressed our heartfelt feelings, which came out spontaneously. And that was the end of our political honeymoon with the Raja. But we do maintain our personal relations with him till date.

Chandra Shekhar Takes Over

After the fall of V.P. Singh Government Chandra Shekhar came into power. But he could not stay any longer as the Congress headed by Rajiv Gandhi withdrew its support. So the ninth Lok Sabha did not serve its full term and the House was dissolved on 12th March 1991, when Chandra Shekhar tendered his resignation from the office of Prime Minister. Chandra Shekhar continued as caretaker Prime Minister till 21st June 1981, when P.V. Narasimha Rao took over as the next Prime Minister after the results of the 10th Lok Sabha elections were declared. Happily the government headed by Narasimha Rao completed its full term, and he continued as such till 16th May 1996. The term of tenth Lok Sabha was upto 8th July 1996. The general elections to the eleventh Lok Sabha were held in 27th April 1986. The term of Narasimha Rao was full of scandals and scams, and the people again were utterly disgusted from the Congress misrule. Criminalisation of politics was at its peak during the tenure of Narasimha Rao. The PIL (Public Interest Litigation) was the order of the day since almost all the institutions failed to work and look into the burning problems of the people.

In the 11th Lok Sabha Elections the people gave a fractured mandate and made it very difficult for any party to form the government. BJP being the largest single party, got the first opportunity to form the government. Atal Bihari Vajpayee was thus administered the oath of Prime Minister on 16th May 1996. Since he could not prove his majority, he tendered his resignation. As per the normal practice, the President asked Mr. Vajpayee to continue as caretaker Prime Minister till the new government was formed.

The people who gave the fractured mandate had been silently watching these political acrobats. All the other parties, including Congress which was the second largest party could not find out a person who would be named as the next Prime Minister. Politics of 'Joar toar' (expediency) had been started with the sole aim of keeping communal forces out of power. But from among the elected representatives, they could not agree to any one name. Ultimately, a farmer from Karnataka who was then the Chief Minister of the State could be brought around to adorn the highest office. Neither was he the member of Parliament, nor was he willing in the first instance to accept the office. But the 13 parties conclave persuaded him to accept the office of Prime Minister. He was thus administered the oath of the office of Prime Minister on Ist June, 1996. Therefore the people were given a Prime Minister, whom they never elected. This name could come on surface, after the formation of the United Front. The top most names for this office were, V.P. Singh, Jyoti Basu, G.K. Moopanar, Ram Krishna Hegde and Laloo Prasad Yadav. H.D. Deve Gowda was thus the last choice of the United Front, which was forced on the electorate most undemocratically and against all norms and values cherished by our forefathers.

The marriage of convenience could not last long on account of infighting and mud slinging among the various constituents. The Congress party which had offered support from outside, also felt completely ignored and ultimately pulled down government headed by H.D. Deve Gowda. The Parliament debates are a witness to the humiliation and condemnations inflicted upon Deve Gowda in person, and the United Front Government in general, while bringing a no confidence motion against the government. After a span of 11 months, the government headed by H.D. Deve Gowda therefore, met its doom and lost the vote of confidence on the Floor of the House.

Old Wine in New Bottle

The Congress Party, second largest with 140 members or so was the deciding factor, whether to seek fresh election or form a government to avoid election. After having meetings of the working committee and serious deliberations, the Congress Party headed by Sita Ram Kesari finally came to the conclusion, that the fresh election should be avoided. They then pin pointed a pliable person, I.K. Gujral, who was the Foreign Minister in Deve Gowda's Govt. and told the United Front leaders, that the Congress could give outside support, if Shri I.K. Gujral was made the Prime Minister.

Without going into detail, it is sufficient to mention here that the name of I.K. Gujral was cleared by the United Front. The Congress party thus addressed a letter to the President offering outside support to the United Front, and the President Shri K.R. Narayanan administered an oath of office of the Prime Minister to Shri I.K. Gujral. The Congress party had cordial relations with I.K. Gujral. His government, therefore, went on smoothly for some time.

Jain Commission Report Turns the Tables

The dramatic release of interim report of Jain Commission alleging the hand of DMK in the assassination of Rajiv Gandhi, turned the tables. Sita Ram Kesari, the Congress President, demanded the head of three DMK ministers, who were in Gujral Government but the Gujral Government firmly decided not to oblige the Congress Party. The Government, in turn asked the Congress party to first have discussions on the report before any decision was taken to remove those ministers. Ultimately the Congress Party withdrew its support from Gujral Government and sent a letter of withdrawal of support from Government addressed to the President. The result was that the 11th Lok Sabha, also came to an end within less than two years of existence and the country was once again pushed into elections for a fresh mandate by the Indian voter.

Before we end this chapter, let us have a quick look of the events that took place in the year 1997.

January 9, 1997: Congress (I) leader N.D. Tiwari and Arjun Singh return to Congress (I).

February 10: The Shiromani Akali Dal Ally BJP sweeps assembly elections in Punjab with 90 seats in the 117 member house.

March 12: Cabinet extends President's rule in U.P.

March 18: Former Union Minister Kalpanath Rai jailed for ten years for harbouring Dawood Ibrahim aids.

March 21: Ms. Mayawati becomes Utter Pradesh's Chief Ministers under a six month power sharing formula between the BJP and BSP.

March 30: Congress (I) Sita Ram Kesari withdraws support to Mr. Deve Gowda's United Front Government.

April 20: Mr. I.K. Gujral sworn in as Prime Minister of the UF Government.

May 8: Mrs. Sonia Gandhi enrolls as Primary Congress (I) member.

May 29: Mr. Rajesh Pilot and Sharad Pawar file papers to contest the Congress (I) Presidential Polls, while Sharad Yadav enters fray for the top most in Janata Dal.

June 13: Mr. Sita Ram Kesari elected President of the Congress (I) in polls, the first in 14 years.

June 18: Bihar Governor, A.R. Kidwai sanctions prosecution of Chief Minister Laloo Prasad Yadav in fodder scam while Mr. Gujral seek resignation of two union ministers accused in the scam.

July 7: Sharad Yadav elected the Janata Dal President.

July 25: Mr. K.R. Narayanan becomes the first Dalit President of India.

July 26: Laloo Prasad resigns and installs Rabri Devi Chief Minister.

August 14: Parliament re-enacts 'freedom at midnight'.

August 16: Mr. Krishan Kant elected Vice President.

August 26: Parliament begins special four day session to discuss development strategy for the next century.

August 28: Election Commission bars convicts from contesting polls from contesting polls notwithstanding a pending appeal in a higher court. Jain Commission submits its 17-volume interim report.

August 29: The Delhi High Court cancels allotment of petrol pumps by Mr. Satish Sharma under Minister's discretionary powers.

September 12: The High Court directs Narasimha Rao and 18 others to face trial in JMM bribery case.

September 21: Kalyan Singh assumes charge as Chief Minister, Uttar Pradesh.

October 20: BSP withdraws support to Kalyan Singh government, but he succeeds to prove his majority in Vidhan Sabha.

October 23: The Central Government forced to backtrack on Central rule in Uttar Pradesh after the President asks it to reconsider its decision.

November 16: Press leaks of Jain Commission Report triggers political upheaval as the Congress (I) seeks the ouster of DMK Minister.

November 28: Mr. Gujral submits resignation to President.

December 4: President dissolves 11th Lok Sabha.

December 11: Laloo Prasad secures bail and decides to form an alternative secular front with Congress I, SP. and BSP.

December 12: Congress (I) leaders Krishna Sahi and Jagannath Mishra quit party.

December 15: Orissa JD splits with 29 members forming Biju Janata Dal.

December 25: Four former Congress (I) ministers join the BJP while the Congress (I) expel rebel leader Mamta Bannerji.

December 26: Gujarat Assembly dissolved after split in Mr. Vaghela's RJP and political uncertainty.

December 30: Sonia Gandhi declares that she would actively campaign for Congress in the Lok Sabha elections—Jubilations in the Congress circles.

SONIA GANDHI—The Saviour

The Congress Party gets a new life with the emergence of Sonia Gandhi, actively participating in the day-to-day affairs of the political happenings inside and outside the country. On 28th November, 1997, Shri I.K. Gujral, submitted his resignation to the President of India. And on 4th December, 1997, the President dissolved the Lok Sabha and directed the Election Commission to hold fresh elections for the 12th Lok Sabha. The Congress party at that time was in very bad shape. The Bharatiya Janata Party was sure to have a cake walk over during the general elections, as the Congress leadership had virtually lost its credibility for variety of reasons. The only hope the Congress at that time had was in Sonia Gandhi. And for quite a long time they had been persuading her to come out of the shell and take the reins of the party in her own hands. It is a known fact that Sita Ram Kesri was too unequal to the august office of the President of the Indian National Congress. The Congress leaders saw the rout of the party on the wall, if the elections were fought under his leadership.

Sonia Gandhi was watching the situation very closely and was convinced that if she did not come out openly and actively, the Congress party would certainly meet its waterloo. Although, a little later (30-12-97) when Sonia Gandhi ultimately declared that she would actively campaign for the Congress party in the 12th Lok Sabha general elections, there were jubilations all over the country, in the Congress circles.

Immediately after her declaration, Sonia Gandhi undertook intensive touring all over the country canvassing for the victory of the Congress candidates. Her presence and active participation in the election campaign did show the desired results. It is a known fact that but for her active participation, the Congress party could not have touched three figures even.

Sonia Takes Over as President of the Congress Party

After her charismatic performance, in the Lok Sabha elections, there was a serious move to remove the Congress President, Sita Ram Kesri, who was nothing but a big liability for the party. Sita Ram Kesri on the other hand, was not inclined to oblige Sonia Gandhi and wanted to stick on the post as long as possible. But the pressure mounted from all quarters, and ultimately, on 14th March, 1998, the Congress Working Committee exercised special powers and removed Sita Ram Kesri from the office of the President of Indian National Congress. In his place, Mrs. Sonia Gandhi was appointed the next President of the Congress Party. On 16th March, Mrs. Gandhi formally took over as Congress Parliamentary Party Chief. The Congress Constitution was amended, and Sharad Pawar was appointed the Congress Party's leader in the Lok Sabha and Manmohan Singh in the Rajya Sabha.

Sonia's Programme Defies Everyone

After Sonia Gandhi took over as the Congress President, her performance and style of functioning had been applauded by one and all. Even her adversaries acknowledged this fact. She was slowly and steadily streamlining the Congress party, and had opened the doors for all those who had left the party for one reason or the other.

At the age of 52, Sonia Gandhi is indeed young enough to learn and old enough to lead. Sonia's electric campaigning leading upto the general elections in 1998, as also the assembly elections, in four States, including the National Capital Territory of Delhi is an indication of her capacity to work with seriousness. Sonia had waited patiently for seven years after the assassination of her husband and has ultimately assumed political responsibilities.

According to Harish Gupta (India Today, 9.11.98) 'For everything that is true of Congress, the opposite is also true. Fresh evidence of this great Nehruvian paradox is provided by the ongoing Assembly Election campaign in Rajasthan, Delhi, Madhya Pradesh and Mizoram. At one level, the Congress is battling for a provincial mandate, attacking the performance of BJP Government in two states and defending its own record in the two other.

That never, is not Sonia Gandhi's perception. The Congress President has converted these local polls into a national contest between Atal Behari Vajpayee and herself—and a referendum on the performance of the BJP led government.'

Mrs. Gandhi's Methods

Sonia is treating these polls as a referendum on Vajpayee the Prime Minister.

In Delhi and Rajasthan, this strategy will be added to the ruling BJP's poor record.

In Madhya Pradesh, it will neutralise State level anti incumbency feelings. If competitive politics is presented as 'Sonia-Atal', tussle, the Congress will upstage the third force.

Should every assembly poll become a vote on Vajpayee, the BJP will be ever nervous.

The Pachmari Meet

Sonia Gandhi called for a 'Narora Type' camp at Pachmari, and set the agenda for her party. It was there that she decided that instead of going in for alliance with any third front, the Congress should build itself up at the state level and concentrate on winning back its traditional base.

Assembly Elections

The agenda which was set by Sonia Gandhi at Pachmari did bear definite fruits during the recent assembly elections, held on 25.11.98 in four States, Delhi, Rajasthan, Madhya Pradesh and Mizoram. Her policy of wait and watch vis-a-vis the Central Government also wins the Congress anti-incumbency benefits. This is her first electoral test after taking over as party president.

Pachmari Declaration at a Glance

1. Coalition will be considered only when absolutely necessary on the basis of agreed programmes which will not weaken the party.
2. Oppose all moves to dilute reservation for SC/ST, OBCs minorities.
3. Commits itself to the substantially enhanced representation of women at all echelons in the party organisation and in distribution of tickets for elections to the State assemblies and parliament.
4. Those party members having more than two children after January, 2000 to be denied party tickets.
5. Decides to appoint a committee to examine electoral reforms with special reference to curbing use of money and muscle power in elections.
6. To accord high priority to evolution of a policy which will treat river waters as a national asset to be used and developed as national grid.
7. To accord highest priority to revival and renewal of the party in Uttar Pradesh, Bihar, West Bengal and Tamil Nadu.
8. Middle path on economic policy, to strengthen subsidies while committing itself to performance assessed at realization of growth rate of 7 to 8 percent per annum. Urges revival of investment and employment opportunities.

AICC Session

Sonia Gandhi, the Congress President gets the AICC nod to usher in a sweeping rewamp in the party. At the end of the day long AICC session on 18.12.98, the party decided to reserve 33% of all posts for women, and 20% for Dalits, Tribals, OBCs and minorities.

"Our work does not end with this", declared Mrs. Sonia Gandhi with a sense of satisfaction. "This is just one more mile stone. We must recruit and train women and others from the weaker sections to fill the reserved posts."

The AICC also okayed a three year term for all party positions and gave her a free hand to reconstitute all bodies—right from the CWC to the PCCs.

Mrs. Gandhi said that the country had been ravaged by the ruling coalition's non governance and that the Congress was ready to discharge its 'constitutional responsibilities' if the situation so demanded. Reiterating her position, Mrs. Sonia Gandhi said, 'while we welcome the support of like-minded parties, we must stand on our own post'. The party must aim to provide a stable government "on our own".

Before the close of the year 1998, almost all the national newspapers, as also a number of journals and magazines have carried stories on the overall performance of Sonia Gandhi after she took over as the Congress President. We take the liberty of reproducing two stories (courtesy: *Hindustan Times* and *Hindu*) which deal with her dynamic performance on all fronts bringing the Congress Party on rails with a bright future in times to come.

Congress's New Mantra: Sonia and Decent Politics

A year ago when Mrs. Sonia Gandhi stepped out of a self-imposed exile to salvage the Congress, the party was ravaged by desertions and internal rivalries during the leadership of her predecessors in the post of Congress President, Mr. P.V. Narasimha Rao and Mr. Sitaram Kesri.

Congressmen were resigned to the prospect of an electoral debacle in the General Elections and handing over the reins of power to the Bharatiya Janata Party, which was then the rising star on India's political horizon, on a platter, as it were.

Mainly due to her leadership, the Congress, which had acquired an infamy of sorts for its numerous acts of expediency, is now swearing by her new mantra: No shortcuts to power.

Mrs. Gandhi has been instrumental in instilling among Congressmen a new sense of purpose and unity, besides creating a new image of a mature party in no tearing hurry to seize power, but confident that it would run the next Government. Congressmen, keen to adhere to her style, now-a-days talk of decent politics, ethics in Government and accountability.

Today, riding the crest of popularity, following the Congress' spectacular wins in the Assembly polls in Delhi, Rajasthan and Madhya Pradesh, Mrs. Gandhi has taken the initiative in changing male domination in political parties by ushering in 33 per cent reservation for women in all posts in Congress and 20 per cent for the Dalits, tribals and the minorities.

By challenging the established male and caste order, she believes she can create a new vote-bank for the Congress.

More than six months ago when she took over as the party chief, she said she was no saviour and the party could not be revived without hard work.

As the year closes, she has almost got the electorate to turn towards the Congress, and to perceive the party as one that alone could govern.

Congress Back in the Reckoning

It is virtually a rags to riches story for the Congress in 1998 which saw a hesitant Ms. Sonia Gandhi being catapulted to the centre stage thereby infusing a fresh lease of life into the 113-year old enervated organisation.

Gasping for breath after dissolution of the eleventh Lok Sabha, following a series of desertions and uncertain electoral prospects, the Congress then led by the old guard Mr. Sitaram Kesri had almost given up hope in the face of an upbeat BJP.

However, Ms. Sonia Gandhi's decision in the midst of the poll battle to campaign for the party had an electrifying effect that helped the Congress to overcome its despondency.

Though the party ended as runners-up in the mid-term polls which threw up a hung verdict, her taking over the stewardship from a reluctant Mr. Kesri, who in an unprecedented development was virtually sacked by the working committee, came as a boon.

Mr. Kesri's downfall was as sudden as his rise to the top party post some two years back when he was handed over the baton by Mr. P.V. Narasimha Rao following his being chargesheeted in a court case.

The moment of glory for Ms. Sonia Gandhi came as the year was drawing to a close as she led the party to a spectacular victory in the Assembly elections to Delhi, Rajasthan and Madhya Pradesh.

The drubbing of the BJP in the poll battle dramatically altered the national political scene reviving hopes within the Congress that power at the Centre was only one step away.

Soon after the Assembly poll verdict, a triumphant Ms. Sonia Gandhi consolidated her hold over the party as she was authorised by an AICC session in Delhi on December 18 to make changes in the organisation at various levels.

In another move to widen the party's support base, she ensured approval for a proposal to provide a combined 20 per cent reservation for the SC, ST, minorities and the OBC thereby making Congress the first national party to reserve as much as 53 per cent of posts for the weaker sections.

The change of mood in the party was abundantly reflected in the session which saw partymen debunking any thought of electoral alliances and vociferously advocating the need for the organisation in providing a stable Government on its own.

Partymen were now looking at Ms. Sonia Gandhi as the future Prime Minister of the country.

Despite being emboldened by the Assembly results and findings of opinion polls that the Congress could win as many as 300 seats in the Lok Sabha in the event of a mid-term poll, the party appeared to tread a cautious path giving indications that it was not for toppling the Vajpayee Government.

This led to the party incurring the wrath of Opposition parties like the Samajwadi Party-Rashtriaya Janata Dal combine which has been insisting that the Congress take a lead in the formation of an alternative Government at the Centre.

An impression started gaining ground among the Opposition parties that the Congress was now interested in coming to power on its own through a snap poll. This perception brought division in the Opposition camp with the SP leader, Mr. Mulayam Singh Yadav, branding the Congress as 'enemy number one'.

The good showing of the Congress in Agra East Assembly by-election was a cause for cheer for the party, but political observers differed on its likely impact in the key state of Uttar

Pradesh, where the organisation has been out of reckoning for nearly a decade.

The win in Adampur Assembly by-election in Punjab as also the victory in Bihar and Maharashtra Legislative Council elections was being seen in the party as a sign of its recovering lost ground.

Just a few months before the Assembly polls, Ms. Sonia Gandhi, much against the advice of senior partymen, held a brainstorming session of party leaders at Pachmari in Madhya Pradesh which came out with a declaration aimed at reviving and revitalising the organisation.

Revival of the party in Uttar Pradesh, Bihar, West Bengal and Tamil Nadu was top on the agenda following Pachmari deliberations in the first week of September.

In the Lok Sabha polls earlier in the year, the party had failed to open its account in Uttar Pradesh which sends 85 MPs and similar was the situation in Tamil Nadu where the party's trusted ally the AIADMK gave it a jolt by siding with the BJP.

Rebellion by Ms. Mamata Banerjee, in West Bengal led to parting of ways by the fiery leader who formed the Trinamool Congress and in the Lok Sabha polls, the Congress had to be content with only one seat—Malda.

Only five Congress MPs won from Bihar, once the party stronghold, and that too mainly because of an alliance with the RJD led by Mr. Laloo Prasad Yadav.

Mrs. Sonia Gandhi who took over the leadership soon after the polls went about the task of setting the house in order in right earnest following an AICC session on April 6 ratifying the CWC decision appointing her as the party chief.

She brought in the former Speaker, Mr. P.A. Sangma as also senior leaders, Mr. Rajesh Pilot and Mr. Sushilkumar Shinde on the CWC and made Mr. Sangma head of a high-level party task force to suggest ways and means to revitalise the organisation. She also appointed several committees to go into the causes of electoral setbacks in various states. A committee to suggest changes in the party constitution was constituted under the leadership of Mr. K. Karunakaran.

She hardly made any changes in the AICC general secretaries but abolished the post of vice-president, thereby sacking Mr. Jitendra Prasad who was appointed to the post by Mr. Kesri.

As the 12th Lok Sabha came into being, she replaced Mr. Kesri as the chairperson of the Congress Parliamentary Party and later nominated Mr. Sharad Pawar and Mr. Manmohan Singh as leaders of Opposition in Lok Sabha and Rajya Sabha respectively.

Incidentally, the year saw the former Prime Minister, Mr. P.V. Narasimha Rao going into further oblivion as he was denied a ticket for the Lok Sabha from Behrampur in Orissa by an adamant Mr. Kesri, who held Mr. Rao responsible for failure to protect the Babri Masjid in 1992.

In Lok Sabha, the party received an initial setback when Mr. Sangma, its nominee backed by the combined Opposition, lost in the election for the Lok Sabha Speakership as the ruling BJP at the last minute plumped for the TDP candidate, Mr. G.M.C. Balayogi following a deal with the Andhra Pradesh Chief Minister, Mr. Chandrababu Naidu.

But as the year drew to a close the party had its sweet revenge when the BJP was forced to yield the post of Lok Sabha Deputy Speaker to the Congress nominee, Mr. P.M. Sayeed as Ms. Mamata Banerjee and the AIADMK supremo Ms. Jayalalitha favoured a consensus on Mr. Sayeed.

ASSEMBLY ELECTIONS
"Contest between Sonia & Vajpayee"

To take stock of the performance of the Vajpayee Government; clash between the R.S.S. and the style of functioning by BJP, interference by the BJP President Kushabhau Thakre, the debacle of the BJP in four Assembly States, and to decide the future course of action, the Bharatiya Janata Party held the Marathon two-day Session at Bangalore, at the beginning of the New Year. In these two day deliberations, the differences between RSS and BJP, Kushabhau Thakre, L.K. Advani and the Prime Minister Atal Behari Vajpayee came on surface in a very big way. Here are some excerpts from the story carried by the Economic Times of 4th January, 1999, under the caption: *"Don't Cross Lakshman Rekha, BJP Meet Tells RSS"*

BJP, which has been under attack from RSS and its affiliates today returned fire when a powerful section of the party's apex decision making body—the National Executive—asked the saffron body to stop meddling in the affairs of the Government.

The tone and tenor of the counter attack was an expression of the growing unease among a sizeable section of the party over the damage that the double talk on crucial issues has been causing to the BJP Government . . . . Mr. Madan Lal Khurana went several steps ahead and saw in the attacks on the Government a scheme to destablise the Vajpayee Government.

"Some people in the Sangh affiliates are bent upon destablishing the Government", he said.

Elsewhere, BMS Chief Dattopant Thengdi, had described the Government's move as a part of sell out and had called the Finance Minister an *Anarth Mantri*.

Many BJP leaders feel that the offensive against the Prime Minister is prompted by Sangh idologues like Thengdi, who cannot reconcile to the Vajpayee Premiership.

"It is a continuation of the decades long Thengdi, - Vajpayee tussle, which began when Sangh decided against naming Thengdi as Guru Golwarkar's successor. The Sangh opted for Balasaheb Deoras as he had a working relationship with Mr. Vajpayee. Now Thengdi is getting back at Vajpayee", said a Party leader.

Here are the highlights of the political resolution moved in this Session held at Bangalore.

> Any attack on a place of worship is deplorable and cannot be condoned.
>
> Vajpayee's government's performance has no parallels.
>
> Bofors probe should be pursued energetically and the guilty punished.
>
> Assembly poll results not a reflection on Centre's performance.
>
> Problem of illegal migrants should be tackled with greater urgency.

Differences between Vajpayee and Advani

Punjab Kesri of 8th January 1999 carries an indepth story under the caption—*Vajpayee ke Jawab se Karyakarni Sann Reh Gayee* (The Executive was stunned at the reply of Vajpayee). And I quote: Here is an English translation of a relevant paragraph:

> "It is unfortunate that comparisons are being made between Atal Behari Vajpayee and Shri L.K. Advani. A clash of personalities between the two has been created. It is said that Advani was responsible to strengthen the party (Sangathan) and when the time came, Atal Behari Vajpayee was made the Prime Minister. It is also said that Vajpayee was against the taking out of the Rath Yatra. And when the Rath Yatra was started by Advaniji, every one knew that Vajpayee would not participate. Just for formality sake, Atalji would show his face at some places. Even after the completion of the journey of Rath Yatra, the whole battle of the consequences arisen out of the Yatra, was

fought by Advaniji, it is claimed. During that time, Atalji would openly criticise among the friends of his circle, the steps taken by Advaniji. But when the elections came, Atal Behari Vajpayee was projected as the Prime Ministerial candidate."

The whole story carried out by the Punjab Kesri is worth reading. There is a serious charge against Atal Behari Vajpayee that he was mixed up with Narasimha Rao, and involved Advani in a false Hawala Case. After this incident Atal Behari Vajpayee became a suspect in the eyes of the supporters of Shri L.K. Advani.

Assembly Elections

In the earlier chapter I disagreed with the BJP Resolution saying the 'Assembly elections do not reflect the performance of the BJP Government at the centre'. The world knows that the Assembly Elections was a mini referendum and has changed the national political scenerio in the country. The debacle of the BJP in four assembly elections has brought the differences between BJP and the Sangh Parivar in the open. The minorities have come to the conclusion that their protection and safety is with the Congress party alone, as the Regional parties have also started in terms of joining the Congress party. In Delhi alone, the BJP committed Harakari by disgracefully removing Sahib Singh Verma, the duly elected Chief Minister, by a glamorous lady—Sushma Swaraj, who had no roots whatsoever in the capital politics. She was perhaps brought to perform the last rites of the BJP regime in the National Capital Territory of Delhi.

A Mini Referendum

India Today, in its issue of November 9, 1998 carries an interesting and quite informative story by Harish Gupta, under the caption Me v/s You. Agreeing with the views of the author as a coincidence, he successfully makes out a point that the Assembly Elections were in reality a National contest between Sonia and Vajpayee, and is thus a mini referendum. To quote, "For everything that is true of Congress the opposite also is true. Fresh evidence of this great Nehruvian paradox is provided by the ongoing assembly campaign in Rajasthan, Delhi, Madhya Pradesh and Mizoram. At one bench the Congress is battling for a provincial mandate, attacking the performance of BJP Governments in two States, and defending its own record in two others.

That, however, is not Sonia Gandhi's perception. The Congress President has converted these local polls into a national contest between Atal Behari Vajpayee and herself and a referendum on the performance of the BJP led Union Governments. Explains Girija Vyas, party spokesperson, 'State issues are no doubt important, but what about the BJP's so called distinctiveness. Over six months, it has proved to be bogus.'

On October 27, Sonia launched the Congress Rajasthan campaign by attacking the Pokhran explosives at a rally in Bikaner. She was not making off the cuff remarks. Rather it was a calculated attack on the Vajpayee Government which was responsible for 'destroying the national consensus with the nuclear tests'. With this Sonia seemed to be moving away from the party's earlier (admittedly guarded) approval of the nuclear explosives.

Senior party leaders do not see it that way though, says K. Natwar Singh, the party's shadow Foreign Minister as also Chief Minister Designate for Rajasthan: "We are not shifting stands. We are only blaming BJP for the mess created by it after explosions." The Comatose State of the Vajpayee administration will be a feature of the Congress pre-election propaganda.

To Sonia's mind, such a strategy will serve two purposes. One, it will help her establish the Congress supremacy as the principal non BJP force in the country, and dash any hopes that the 'third front' may have nurtured on that account. She wants to convert the election—indeed, she wants to convert Indian politics—into a straight bout between Vajpayee and herself. Thus even State elections will be seen as a clash of the two titans.

During the Assembly elections in the four States, Sonia Gandhi successfully exposed the BJP Government on all fronts and carried the masses with her higher charismatic personality. She really emerged as a lady of masses in these elections. Even in Lok Sabha elections, her active participation made a marked difference.

In a very short span of time, when she came out of 10 Janpath to campaign for the Congress Party she exhibited her political wisdom and nack to hit the BJP, the main adversary at the right point. And I quote, 'A direct link between the BJP's nuclear boast and the common man's woe's was made at Bikaner when Sonia highlighted the fact that 'Pokhran villages lack drinking water', such as roads, power and communications'. There was no information available on the states of Pokhran's water supply in 1974.

The manifesto is merciless. "Skyrocketting prices and a stagnant economy are putting the country into recession". The efforts to 'Indianise' education also finds mention. "Our secular heritage is constantly under threat." Decoded Sonia Gandhi is telling the voters of Rajasthan and Delhi that whether at the Centre or in the States, the BJP is the natural party of misgovernance. In Madhya Pradesh and Mizoram she hopes this sentiment will neutralise the anti-incumbency factor . . . . Sonia will try to make every assembly election—Andhra Pradesh and Karnataka in 1999, Bihar and Maharashtra in 2000—a plebiscite on Atal Raj. Vajpayee will premially be on probation."

The results of all these assembly elections go to prove that it was not a battle at state level, it was in fact, a mini referendum between the two stalwarts, Sonia and Vajpayee."

While coming at the close of the chapter, I came across a very interesting 'Letter to the Editor' highlighting the helplessness and haplessness of the Prime Minister Atal Behari Vajpayee, in expanding his cabinet.

Atal's Dilemma

Once again the BJP and its allies seem to have agreed to disagree. Atal Behari Vajpayee had said very "confidently" that he would expand his cabinet on January 15, perhaps he was not aware of the combined fire power of Mamatadi and Jaya Amma.

This drama of cabinet expansion has consumed tonnes of newsprint and hundreds of minutes on TV channels without producing any results. Cabinet berths seem to be the only way a beleaguered Vajpayee can keep his 'flock' together. Good governance has become "allies management." Bachelor Vajpayee seems to lack the experience of dealing with Bharatiya naris.

Indian Express
16.01.1999

Ajay Chaturvedi

AKALI ANTICS

*Avtar Singh Sohal**

The hallowed Sikh doctrine of inseperability of religion and politics has never been properly understood nor correctly practised. Religion has an effective and positive role to play in the world of sense and form by promoting social harmony, love, equality, freedom and fraternity of whole mankind. Goodness, righteousness, piety, compassion, mercy and forgiveness is the essence of every faith. Sikh Gurus, in their integrated vision envisaged life as one whole and there is no dichotomy between spiritual and empirical or temporal realms of human existence and it cannot be segregated into separate compartments, religion, social, cultural, economical or political.

Sri Aurobindo said "To make all life religion and to govern all activities by the religious idea would seem to be the right way to the development of the ideal individual and ideal society and the lifting of the whole life of man into divine." In every human activity, be it social, political or spiritual adherence to idealism, aestheticism and ethics, ensures a quintessentially an ideal civilised society. But, inspite of religious sanctions, the human history is replete with blood stained and fiery tracks which the religion has left furrowed across the medieval age to the very recent times which militates against the claim of religion to be the directing light and regulating power or ethics.

---

* Advocate, Supreme Court of India, New Delhi.

Man has failed religion by blatantingly defying and demeaning its sublime dictates. If he imbibes the positive postulates, virtues and naunces of spirituality, practises them in thought and deed in every sphere of his action and conducts himself strictly dictated by his conscience, then no one will decry and denounce the concept of combination of religion and politics. A devout religious person always desists from evil and pernicious thought, subjects himself to strict discipline, has piety, forgiveness, endurance, compassion and charity towards less privileged fellow beings. History reveals that the combination of religion and politics was always twisted and distorted. The politics when is used for the affairs of the church or vice-a-versa, it always spelt disaster for the humankind. The religion should not be used as a vehicle for securing political power. The essence and crux of the combination of religion and politics is that while practising politics one should always be ethical, virtuous, honest, conscientious, equitable, compassionate and selfless. One should not assume power for self aggrandisement. But, experience certainly proves that everyman who has power is impelled to abuse it and one tends to say that an honest politician is a rare commodity and difficult to find as it is impossible to find an honest burglar. Windell Phillips said, "The hand entrusted with power, becomes, either from human depravity or esprit de corps, the necessary enemy of the people."

In the contemporary competing political systems, ethics have become more relevant and necessary than before for a harmonious and proper social order. Dr. Mohd. Iqbal lamented on the depravity of human mind without ethics and his words echo even today through this couplet.

"Jamale Patshahi Ho
Ya Jamhoori Tamasha
Juda Ho Deen Se Siyasast
To Rai Jati Hai Changezi"

The pith and substance of the said couplet is that whether there is despotic rule or democratic system, if there are no ethics, it results into Changez Khan's dispensation.

Ascending the summit of power should be through ethical means, imbued with deep sense of service of the people who have reposed trust in their leadership and they should conduct as an honest trustee truthfully and faithfully serves his fiduciaries. But the political climbers often are prone to the vice of turning their eyes away from the problems and begin to look about themselves, dignify meanness and depravity and magnify their littleness to the chagrin, despair and anguish of the ever acquiescent people whom they take for granted. Under the veneer of trusteeship, they plunder and rob the very people who are the source of their sustenance.

The subject which I have chosen is very expansive and wide which cannot be capsuled in this article. I wish there is a debate on the concept of combination of religion and politics, its parameters and limitations, instead of outrightly rejecting it out of hand. Meaningful discussion can prove efficacious in the present appalling circumstances enabling our political class to evolve and adopt some code of conduct based on the positive postulates of spirituality.

Leaving the said concept for some appropriate occassion for threadbare discussion, I confine myself to a topic which very much concerns me personally, as a Sikh and would like to share my thoughts with the readers. I have no hesitation to say that the subject I am broaching is too volatile and explosive which may even earn me wrath and flak from my community leadership. I do not care for that. I do not suffer from herd passivity syndrome and have courage to say what is truthful and right though it may bite anyone. Time has come to stand before a crowd without fear of being debunked or lynched. This I have learnt, after reading the espitle Zafarnama written by the tenth Guru to Aurangzeb the most tyrant emperor in the history of India.

I am a devout Sikh born and brought up in Sikh traditions. I am not *amritdhari*. I have no qualms of conscience for not observing and displaying all the five symbols. Yet I feel myself to be an ardent believer of Sikh teachings. Mere symbolism does not make a true religionlist if one is not endowed with the virtues of being true follower of Sikh faith. Even without all the symbols, I am proud to be a Sikh. The richest heritage of Sikh religion makes me feel one of the most blessed persons in the world. I may reiterate that I feel proud to be

Sikh first, then Punjabi and then Indian. If I say otherwise I would be hypocritical. Before anyone raises eye brows on my unconventional statement, I want to at once assure that, a true Sikh who is follower of Sikh Gurus would quintessentially be Indian, fiercely nationalist, irretrievably committed to the soil and would lay down his life for its security, integrity, freedom, glory and honour of the country. The faith enabled the sikh community to grapple with the diverse grave socio-political challenges over the centuries and acquired a glorious heritage, chivalry sufferings, deprivations, and martyrdoms. It was the Sikhs who after hundreds of years reversed the course of history by forcing the invaders back to their lands and once for all sealed the vulnerable borders in the North-West against all future invasions.

In the current century itself Sikhs played a pioneering role in the freedom struggle out of all proportions to their small population. The first two revolts against the British, Kuka revolt and Ghadr movement were almost wholly manned by sikhs. Out of 2175 martyrs for country's freedom 1557 were Sikhs. Out of 2646 sent to Andaman for life imprisonment 2147 were Sikhs. INA led by Bose had 60% of Sikhs. During emergency, maximum number of agitators jailed were Sikhs. In economic field Sikhs brought about green and white revolutions.

The raison d'etre behind the preceding exposition of factual natrix is to allay fear that Sikhs can ever think of entertaining the idea of separation. How can a builder be destroyer? Can a saviour be killer? Answer would be no.

Past two decades have been most traumatic and nightmarish for Sikhs. We lost our identity and image. We were being dubbed as secessionists. We became suspects in the eyes of the nation. The glorious and most impeccable credentials of the community got blurred. I feel overwhelming sense of deja-vu and rather shame when I think and analyse the genesis of the events culminating in loss of respect and credibility. Who is responsible to cause dent on our credibility? If I am to hold anyone guilty I would squarely indict the Sikh leadership. I feel proud to assert without fear of contradiction that my community is one of the most prosperous, dynamic, chivalrous, adventurous and civilized races of the world. But the darkest side of the community is its leadership. It is woefully medieval and feudal, retrogade, depraved, visionless, untrust-worthy and fossilised. The leadership provided by Chiefs of twelve confederacies which Sikhs resolved themselves was better than the present Sikh leadership. Fortunately there was Maharaja Ranjit Singh who consolidated these fragmented and disarrayed feudal dispensations into a well knit conclave and under his able leadership an empire was built. But, it is a sad plight when we need a powerful person like Maharaja, there is none to whom we can look for, stewardship. There is no silver lining. No ray of hope. This is the bane of the community that we are moving like rudderless ship navigating through troubled waters. Lions are being led by donkeys.

When Akali party is in power, they fight among themselves and have always utterly failed to provide ideal administration. Governance, perhaps is not their forte. Their terms of Governments were always incomplete and due to their own misdemeanour used to be cut short. It is intriguing to notice that whenever they are at the helms of affairs they never address to any problem, issue or demands which were begging solution. Past history reveals that whenever they had lost power they would launch agitation in the name of panth and throw people into vortex of chaotic situation. Due to lack of skill, direction, vision to combat crisis they fail to manage pell mell created by their own antics. Who suffers? We the sikhs who are apolitical and particularly who live outside Punjab.

Adverting to the present Akali leadership it is irony of fate, that they have once again captured the reins of Government. Their past dossiers deserved for them place in the dustbin of history. They are men of no sterling substance who have not imbibed even a modicum of ethics which their religion has taught them and particularly when ad nauseam they profess that religion and politics are inseparable. They have rubber spines and feet of clay. Where were they when the Punjab in general and Sikhs in particular needed direction, guidance and help to extricate itself from the throes of terrorism and the prevailing unsettled conditions? They made themselves, scarce. This coterie which has manipulated power and is part of centre administration also. Now after coming into power there is not even a whisper about the demands for which they had been fighting. Since they are partners in the Union Govt., they are in a position to effectively secure permanent solutions of water dispute, transfer of Chandigarh and Punjabi speaking territories etc. Is there any explanation for inaction on their part?

Intellectuals are always considered last bastion of the communities whose able guidance extricate them from critical situations. But sikh intellectuals are worst than the rugged politicians. Sikh intellectuals are having price tags on their lapels and can be bought a dime a dozen. Before the recent Delhi Assembly elections an assortment of intellectuals assuming themselves to be sole arbiters and self appointed guardians of fate and faith of the Delhi Sikhs issued a dictate prohibiting us from aligning with Congress. This was most unwise, untimely, unwarranted and unsolicited advice. This coterie included retired Sikh judges. This was most unbecoming of such hify dignitaries. Judges by virtue of their training, traditions and background should not indulge in cheap gimmicks which reflects upon their credibility. My experience tells me that Sikh intellectuals try to exploit their minority card and stoop low to secure plum posts and once they are secured in their saddles they do nothing for the community. Rather, they feel proud to demonstrate indifference to their brethren to establish their secular and liberal credentials and even normal discretion to which his fellow Sikh is entitled is denied to him. A Sikh lawyer who was not found fit to be a high Court Judge used Sikh minority tag and secured a berth in the apex court. But worst sufferers were Sikh lawyers at his hands. After demitting office, he is dabbling in Sikh politics and busy in projecting as the future Chief Minister. He for ulterior objects has constituted people's commission in which he has roped in a Sikh retired High Court Judge also.

It is intriguing that a Judge retired on 17th July 1998 and sat in the Commission on 8th August 98. When was he taken into confidence for being included in the commission? Obviously when he was still in office. Such conduct does not bring glory or respect to such individuals.

Enough is enough. Politics can no more be left to the politicians. Our community should make concerted efforts to regain the lost glory, image and credibility. We have to assure the nation that we can have disputes, difference of opinion or disagreements with individuals or parties but we can not destroy the nation.

In our democratic polity which is composed of multireligious, multiethnic and multilingual groups we cannot afford a state which has theocratic agenda and is not founded on secular principles. The present dispensation has started controversy between majority and minorities. This is perilous. It has to be curbed. Sooner the better. Secular forces should rally around Congress under the leadership of Mrs. Sonia Gandhi to stem the onslaught on secular character and fabric of our polity. Congress is not a fiefdom it is an institution which must be strengthened.

Sikhs have to forget the past and redefine the role in the changed circumstances. Our alliance with die hard Hindu communalists is unsustainable. They try to use us by reminding us about the 1984 massacre. Congress has shown and expressed regrets. We have to believe them once again. We are deeply religious people, believe in humanism and shun rabid fanaticism. Then how can we have nexus with Sangwalas? Again Sikh leadership which is driving us in wrong direction should be disassociated with. My outbursts are not frenzied, they are tranquil well reasoned and mature reaction.

Shah Mohd's lament exclaimed by him at the collapse of the Sikh empire, echos even today. *Shah Mohammad Ek Sarkar Bajo Faujan Jit Ke Ant Nu Harian Ne.* Victorious troops lost battle in the absence of the 'Sarkar'. Is it not apt and prophetic even today?

ATAL BEHARI VAJPAYEE
(P.M. in Chains)

The March, 1998 12th Lok Sabha Elections did not give a clear mandate to any single political party. The Bharatiya Janata Party emerged as the single largest party and the Congress came next to BJP.

After the results were declared, hectic efforts were made to prevent BJP to form the Government at the Centre. Every constituent put forward its demands in one way or the other. Some parties agreed to join the Government, while few offered their issue based support from outside. Ultimately on 15th March, 1998 the President invited Atal Behari Vajpayee to form the Government. On 19th March, 1998, Shri Vajpayee took over as the Prime Minister, heading the BJP led Government coalition, which released a 35 point national agenda for governance, a day earlier. He was sworn in alongwith 43 other members of his cabinet. From day one Sushiri Jaya Lalitha, created difficulties for smooth running of the Govt. on one pretext or the other. She even delayed the letter of support to the BJP led Government addressed to the President of India. This created a bad taste in every body's mouth.

On 23rd March, 1998 Chandrababu Naidu, Chief Minister of Andhra Pradesh pulled out of the United Front. And his party fielded G.M.C. Balayogi as a nominee for office of the Speaker for a quid pro quo. The BJP and other allies elected him the Speaker of the Lok Sabha on 25th March, 1998. On 28th March, 1998, Vajpayee Government thus won the Vote of Confidence with last minute support of the Telgu Desam Party.

Under these circumstances, the BJP led Government with the support of 18 parties belonging to different ideologies started its innings.

Pokhran II

Under the leadership of Atal Behari Vajpayee, India flexed its nuclear muscle by exploding three devices underground in the Pokhran Range of Rajasthan, on 11th May, 1998. The Govt. declared that this exercise had been undertaken keeping in view its policy of acquiring nuclear capability. On 13th May, 1998, India conducted two more similar tests in the Pokhran Range. After conducting these tests, India reiterated its offer to consider accepting some of the provisions of the Comprehensive Test Ban Treaty. On 15th May BJP led government declared India as a Nuclear Weapon State.

The Vajpayee Government earned bouquets and brickbats for this adventure. But one thing is certain that the secrecy successfully maintained was excellent. Rather it failed all the Intelligence Agencies of the World.

Debate in Parliament

There was a marathon debate in Parliament on the pros and cons of these explosions. The whole debate has been highlighted in our Book—POKHRAN II—published by Regency Publications. The debate took place on 27th May, 1998, with the opening speech by Atal Behari Vajpayee followed by the Speakers from different political parties. In his opening speech, Prime Minister said, "Sir, I rise to inform the House of momentous developments that have taken place while we were in recess. On 11th May, India successfully carried out three underground nuclear tests. Two more under-ground tests on 13th May completed the planned series of tests. I would like this House to join me in paying fulsome tributes to our scientists, engineers, and defence personnel whose singular achievements have given us a renewed sense of national pride and self confidence.

In 1947, when India emerged as a free country to take its rightful place in the comity of nations, the nuclear age had already dawned . . . . During the fifties India took the lead in calling for an end to all nuclear weapon testing. Addressing the Lok Sabha on 2nd April, 1954, Pandit Jawaharlal Nehru to whose memory we pay homage today stated, "nuclear chemical and biological energy and power should not be used to forge weapons of mass destruction." . . . .

Our decision not to sign the NPT was in keeping with our basic objectives. In 1974, when Smt. Indira Gandhi was the Prime Minister, we demonstrated our nuclear capability. Successive Governments thereafter have taken all necessary steps in keeping with that resolve and national will, to safeguard India's nuclear option. This was the primary reason behind the 1996 decision for not signing the CTBT, a decision that also enjoyed the consensus of this House . . . . Our Nuclear Policy has been marked by restraint and openness. We have not violated any international agreement either in 1974, or now, in 1998. The restraint exercised for 24 years, after having demonstrated our capability in 1974, is in itself a unique example. Restraint, however, has to arise from strength. It cannot be based upon indecision or doubt . . . . To the people of India, and Indians abroad, I convey my profound gratitude.

We look to the people of India and Indians abroad, for support in the difficult period ahead.

Shri Inderjit Gupta

So, Sir, I must say more or less in conclusion that the whole exercise appears to me to have been an exercise in futility . . . . "

K. Natwar Singh

As far as the Congress Party is concerned, our views on the subject have been made clear in this Congress Working Committee met on 14th of May, and endorsed the statement of the Congress President, Smt. Sonia Gandhi which reads as follows:

> "I would like to place on record, in this formal meeting of the Working Committee, the pride we feel in the achievement of our nuclear scientists and engineers who are putting India's nuclear capability in the front rank. We recall with equal pride the successive Congress govern-

ments have ensured India's nuclear capability remains upto date so that our security is not compromised .... The Congress Party remains committed to a nuclear - weapon free world and that remains the sheet anchor of our policy."

Shri G.M. Banatwala

Sir, Pakistan has detonated its nuclear to dissuade Pakistan from doing so. This is a dangerous situation. I only hope that it does not lead to any race for nuclear weapons. Happily, our Prime Minister has said in his own statement and I quote: "We do not intend to engage in arm race."

.... I conclude by saying that really a policy of consensus should be followed and it is only through this policy that the country will be able to stand united and will be able to face any challenge that may come before us."

After the Pokhran II explosions, the BJP led Governments faced many hurdles and difficulties in the day to day running of the Government. It is just not possible to mention in detail all the incidents, as it requires an independent book to highlight all the events. But we shall try to highlight in brief, what prevented Vajpayee Govt. to deliver goods and provide able and stable government.

Political Uncertainty

The year 1998 started with the country holding its breath for that new great hope—Atal Behari Vajpayee. It ended with opinion polls pointing the fingers of expectation at another new great hope—Sonia Gandhi. It began with enormous expectations at the formation of India's first genuine non-Congress Government. It concluded with the same sentiment being transferred back to the Congress. For the people of India 1998 has been a rollercoaster ride with exhilarating ups and treacherous lows. And the stomach is still churning.

From day one when Vajpayee took over as Prime Minister, Mamata and Jaya Lalitha the most vocal and trouble shooter allies kept him on his toes, in one way or the other.

He had to despatch his emissaries to Chennai quite often to keep Jaya Lalitha in good humour. India Today has aptly described the plight of Vajpayee Govt. in its 4th January issue. And I quote: "It happened all too fast Vajpayee scraped through the election but did not have to wait even a single day for political uncertainty to begin. The indefatigable Jaya Lalitha made sure that he did not have the luxury of even celebrating his victory. Nor was she alone. The Prime Minister did not have even to wait one day for his first political casualty. Jaswant Singh's name was submitted to the President as a Minister-in-waiting. In a midnight coup he fell by the way-side. He became India's first non-ex-minister-in-waiting. Eight months later he was back in business.

It was also a fast moving year that was entirely dominated by politics. Within a month of Vajpayee taking over, there were the nuclear tests in Pokhran. Stung by their own audacity the people celebrated and gloated at the headlines of gate-crashing into the world's most exclusive club. They were premature celebrations. Faced with the twin problems of international ostracism and internal confusion, the high of the N-tests were quickly followed by the low of their fall out. We began 1998, not knowing where the country was heading. We closed December exactly the same place. Yet in less than 12 months we had travelled through almost the entire gamut of oppositions. Without resolving our confusions."

The Indian Express in its editorial called it "The year of unreason". Here are some excerpts. It was not in Sanskrit that India endorsed the arrival of BJP as a party of governance. It arrived in Delhi not in a chariot adorned with comic book mythology. The triumph of the BJP as the single largest party was the culmination of degeneration elsewhere in the political market. The Congress like the liberal democrats of Japan was decaying with the memories of power, with the self-repudiation leadership. The Janata with its social therapy subordinated force of irrelevance. A BJP led coalition in power marked the right turn in Indian politics. That human face, like Dubeck from the Parivar, was also most popular face. But there was no romance of the arrival. Those who received the mandate failed to realise its historic resonance. There was no end-of the-era glow in their eyes, no word of change in their vocabulary. The acts of coalition, with India's most popular politician as its Manager, ranged from the banal to the bizzare.

The BJP's most significant national statement was singularly bombastic. A nuclear policy based on national assertion and international responsibility exhibited political maturity. The funny thing was that nuclear India could not manage its vegetable markets. Symbols and gestures are no substitutes for good governance . . . . In India 1998 churches burned to illuminate the politics of hate. The torch bearers of civilisation wanted to regain the ancient land. The self chosen culture cleanser was the most active personality of the year..... One India kept forward with the immense confidence of a modern nation. It struck a final balance between power and responsibility. The other India sought out the great yesterday, which in the hallucinations of the so called civilisational man looked so archaic, so ancient, so exclusive.

The great yesterday had another manifestation. The Congress party thinks it is India's natural party of governance. In 1998 the party realised that it was not biologically or intellectually capable of managing the future India. Sonia Gandhi, for long the extra-Constitutional the Mother India, found herself soaring above the dead minds of India's GOP Political necrophilia collaborated with intimations of morality to turn the first widow into the Supreme Leader. It was the triumph of the dynastic impulse. The year legitimised the inevitability of a Gandhi in the Congress. The term 'end of the Congress Century" was quite popular sometime ago. Mrs. Gandhi had arrived, and after life was a possibility. Perhaps Sonia Gandhi was not the singular source of the Congress regeneration. The overstretched pause of the BJP leadership also provided life saving energy to the other party. The result was not so bad, the first note of a bipartisan polity."

The Enemy Within

In yet another editorial Hindustan Times, exposes successfully that the real remote control is in the hands of the RSS which is interfering too much in smooth functioning of the BJP led coalition government. In this situation, even 100 Vajpayees will not be able to provide able or stable governance, particularly when it is not the BJP government, it is BJP led government with 18 other allies, functioning in accordance with the national agenda agreed to by all the constituents. I quote: "Reports that there were protests, some muffled, some stridently expressed by senior party members against the incessant interference of the Rashtriya Swayam Sevak Sangh in the work of Central Ministries carry anominous message for the Vajpayee Government. Even as the Prime Minister keep pussy-footing the Gujarat Government's attitude towards the Christian minority he must be realising that the real enemy of his government is neither the opposition nor the tantrum throwing allies, but the BJP's ideological fountain-head—RSS.

If there is one person who does represent the moderate face of the BJP, it is Mr. Vajpayee. He has to take the RSS bull by the horn and subdue it."

Differences between BJP and RSS

In its national executive meeting at Bangalore, differences surfaced between the BJP and the RSS supremo. And the line adopted by Vajpayee was accepted and the draft resolution had to be redrafted accordingly. I quote : "The political resolution adopted at the BJP's national executive today formally endorsed Mr. Vajpayee's line and condemned the attacks on Christians in Gujarat, 'Any attack on a place of worship, whether a church or a temple is deplorable and cannot be condoned, it said.'

The political resolution which was redrafted after extensive discussions, rejected the Kushabhau Thakre establishment's stand that conversion was the cause for the trouble in the Dangs district of Gujarat. Mr. Madan Lal Khurana, Parliamentary Affairs Minister, openly blamed the Sangh leadership for their unwarranted interference in the affairs of the goverment. He openly said at the Bangalore meet that he saw in the attack by the Sangh Parivar, on the government a scheme to destablise the Vajpayee establishment." (Economic Times 4.1.1998.) Then what is wrong when Sonia Gandhi says that this government will soon fall under its own weight.

One of the resolutions adopted at the Bangalore Meet was: "Assembly poll results not a reflection on centre's performance." The auther entirely disagrees with this resolution. The future elections will show that it was the performance at the Assembly Elections in the four states, that has damaged the good prospects of the BJP in the Lok Sabha as also Assembly Elections. Sushma Swaraj alone has finished BJP in Delhi in particular and other states in general. We are here to witness the results of the future elections. In the next pages we are reproducing some editorials and media reports, which speak volumes on the poor performance of the BJP. Let the BJP the largest single party learn a lesson from history, and face the realities of the events. The party may be very good in opposition, but it has certainly failed to govern in providing an able and stable government. In the Congress party, there is one and only one unquestionable leader. Sonia Gandhi—without any remote control from any quarter, whatsoever as against Atal Behari Vajpayee, who is in chains, facing his own President, Kashubhau Thakre and 18 other allies, who have made his life miserable. He has not been able to have his team of ministers, which is entirely his prerogative. About a year has passed away, he still is not having a complete cabinet. These are the hazards of a coalition government. He was to expand his cabinet, but Mamata Banerjee has given a threat that in case she does not get Railway Ministry, she would withdraw her support. Even if God comes on earth, he would not be able to provide a smooth governance with this type of coalition partners. Single party rule with a strong opposition is, therefore, the only answer. It is for the voters to take a firm stand and provide a clear mandate in favour of a single party.

Correcting PM Party Equation

We have seen that besides the difficulties faced by Atal Behari Vajpayee from his 18 other allies who are a part and parcel of his government by giving issue-based support from inside and outside, he is also facing a major interference from the BJP President Kushabhau Thakre, which openly came on the surface at the Bangalore Meet. For the first time, after he took over as Prime Minister about a year back, he has shown his mettle and gave a clear signal to the party, that he was not obliged to be guided every now and then, while performing his duties as the Prime Minister of India. Harish Khare, (a political commentator) in Hindu of January 6, has traced out the relations between the Prime Minister and the Party President from the days of Pandit Jawaharlal Nehru in a very lucid manner, which are very much relevant in today's political scenario. I quote.* "The showdown between the Prime Minister, Mr. Atal Behari Vajpayee and the Bharatiya Janata Party President, Mr. Khushabau Thakre, staged at Bangalore, was inevitable; and the outcome, a clear-cut victory for the Prime Minister, is not a surprise. The only surprise is that it came eight months too late. After all, there is an element of built-in institutional antagonism between the head of the parliamentary wing and the organisation boss(es); and, it was perhaps too much of an insistence on the BJP being a "party with a difference" that blinded the senior leaders to the requirement of redefining the relationship between the parliamentary and organisational wings.

Soon after Independence Prime Minister Jawaharlal Nehru faced a similar situation. The then Congress President, Acharya Kriplani believed that the Prime Minister was obliged to consult the party in all matters including cabinet composition and policy initiatives.

The good Acharya had argued: "It is the party from which the Government of the day derives its power. Any notion which weakens the organisation of the party or lower its prestige in the people must sooner or later undermine the position of the Government."

The Nehru-Kriplani equation was as skewed in favour of the Prime Minister as is the Vajpayee-Thakre equation. With active support from his deputy, Sardar Patel, Nehru bluntly turned down Acharya Kriplani's demand for a say in the working of the Government. And being the Englishman that he was, Nehru could cite the precedent of the Atlee-Laski showdown in England only a few years earlier. Nehru pretty much told the party president that it was not possible for the

* By Harish Khare, New Delhi, January 5.

Government to seek the indulgence of the Congress Working Committee every time there was a policy to be finalised.

A thoroughly exasperated Kriplani resigned as Congress President, and soon left the party; but not before the principle of parliamentary autonomy vis-a-vis the organisation got fully established. It also helped that Nehru had no political rivals, inside and outside the party, to show him down.

Later the Nehru-Purshottam Das Tandon spat, and many years later, the Indira Gandhi-K. Kumaraj stand-off ended up reinforcing the principle that the government of the day could not be dictated to in its day-to-day functioning, except in the broadest sense of laying down the political parameters.

The Congress arrangement was to combine in one person the post of the leader of the party and that of the parliamentary wing. During the P.V. Narasimha Rao years the collective wisdom of the party never endorsed the "one man, one post" demand; apart from political calculations, there was an institutional preference that nothing should be done to dilute and weaken the authority of the Prime Minister as the chief political executive of the Indian State. The principle of combining the two offices was reiterated even during Mr. Sitaram Kesri's short-lived innings as it is being practised now, though Mrs. Sonia Gandhi is not even a member of either House of Parliament.

Of course, the principle of "the Prime Minister has the upper hand" took a definite beating during the United Front governments; both Mr. Deve Gowda and Mr. I.K. Gujral had no option but to function as one among the equals. The "Steering Committee" emerged as the super-cabinet: and, when Mr. Gujral was chosen to replace Mr. Gowda, he was happy to allow the United Front bosses to select his cabinet for him. Political correctness was redefined to suggest that perhaps the country was better off without a strong and stern Prime Minister.

Mr. Vajpayee became the Prime Minister on the slogan of "able leader, stable government"; implicit in the slogan was that the BJP would be able to reverse the trend in the erosion of the prime ministerial authority, which in turn was allowing everyone else—the Judiciary, the Election Commission, the armed forces, the bureaucracy and others—to ignore, if not defy, the institutional authority of the Union Cabinet.

But Mr. Vajpayee too found himself checkmated from day one. He could not have Mr. Jaswant Singh in his cabinet, because the RSS reportedly was averse to the idea of finding a ministerial berth for those who had been defeated only a few weeks ago. Nonetheless Mr. Vajpayee could not shake off the demands, expectations, and interference of the RSS and other hardliners of the Sangh Parivar. The likes of Mr. Thakre and others do have a point when they object to the BJP Government suddenly subscribing to a policy or legislation the party had opposed only a year ago but the compulsions of a coalition cabinet government have their own logic.

Above all, no prime minister—and certainly not a relatively weak Prime Minister like Mr. Vajpayee—can preside over the Union Government and yet ignore the requirements of the Indian State system. It has taken Mr. Vajpayee nine months and three major election defeats to appreciate this inescapable fact; it is now for the RSS and other members of the Parivar, dedicated as they are to the grand objective of steering the polity away from its Nehruvian moorings, to decide whether they want to keep on supporting Mr. Vajpayee as he perforce plays a Jawaharlal Nehru.

SINGLE PARTY RULE IS THE ONLY ANSWER

If we look back to the political history of our country after independence, we will find that so long as there was one party rule, it worked very well. Jawaharlal Nehru had the privilege to adorn the office of Prime Minister right from the independence until he died on May 27, 1964. After his death Lal Bahadur Shastri took the reins of our country. But his tenure was short-lived as he died prematurely and mysteriously in a foreign land. After his death Indira Gandhi came on the scene and she continued to be the Prime Minister of this great country until 1977 in the first span and then from 1980 to 31st October, 1984 when she was killed by her own security guard. Then Rajiv Gandhi was administered an oath of office of the Prime Minister.

First Coalition Government

After emergency was relaxed and the elections were declared by the Government headed by Smt. Indira Gandhi sometime in the month of February, 1977, the Janata Party, consisting of various political parties with different ideologies, fathered by Lok Nayak Jaya Prakash Narayan, and headed by Shri Morarji Desai came into power. At that point of time, when all the leaders gathered at the Raj Ghat, Acharya Kriplani warned the people of our country, that these leaders are men of clay, 'they are not saints or fakirs'; the people are the masters and these leaders are the servants; the public must be vigilant and keep a constant eye on the style of functioning of the government. Acharya's words are very much relevant even in today's political scenario. If we do not empower the last man in the street, the democracy will remain meaningless, farce and sham.

Atal Behari Vajpayee was the Minister of External Affairs; Ch. Charan Singh and Babu Jagjivan Ram ultimately became two Dy. Prime Ministers, Lal Krishan Advani held the portfolio of Information and Broadcasting. We have already discussed the continuous infighting among the different constituents in the earlier chapter of the book. As already mentioned, the one point programme of Janata Party Government was to humiliate and torture Indira Gandhi in one way or the other. Even the father of Janata Party Loknayak Jaya Prakash Narayan felt very much disgusted as the men in power stopped giving any respect and response to his guidance and advice. In fact J.P. died as a very sad man as he saw the dark future of the country at the hands of the Janata Party Government during his life time.

Fall of Janata Party Government

Ultimately after 28 months of its taking over the reins of the country, Janata Party Govt. failed to deliver goods and Morarji Desai, the then Prime Minister tendered his resignation. So, that was the end of the Janata Govt. formed with the combination of different constituents under the patronage of Loknayak Jaya Prakash Narayan. The leaders thus betrayed the faith, aspirations and confidence of the people, who had expected good governance, by the Janata Government. What further happened was more shameful. Amusingly Morarji Desai, after having tendered resignation staked his claim to form the government. And in his over enthusiasm, a false list of supporters was submitted to the President. On the other hand Ch. Charan Singh staked his claim with the assurance of the outside support by Smt. Indira Gandhi. Knowing fully well that this kind of support by the Congress to Ch. Charan Singh, who was arch enemy of Indira Gandhi all through, the President certainly faltered and failed to perform his duty objectively and in the interest of welfare of the people who were wedded to the democratic norms and traditions. It is a sad commentary on the office of the President that with this type of support by the Congress(I), the President went ahead in administering oath of office of Prime Minister to Ch. Charan Singh, having his subjective satisfaction under Art. 75(3) of the Constitution of India.

H.M. Seervai, an eminent constitutional expert has dealt with this most unfortunate and shameful act in his book "Constitutional Law of India". Vol. II, 1984 (Epilogue pp 2706–2728).

Here are some Excerpts:

In para 13 at page 2710 Seervai writes, "It should be mentioned that though Mr. Charan SIngh was loud in his denunciation of Mrs. Gandhi and accused his colleagues in the Ministry of being, "a bunch of impotent men" for not prosecuting her with vigour, he sought the support of Congress (S) which had separated from her party because it could not agree with her authoritarian way. The support sought was that of two hostile parties and as regards the Congress (I) of a party which had made it known day in and day out, that it stood for abolishing the special courts set up by the Janata Government and for withdrawing the prosecution against Mrs. Gandhi was unconditional . . . . It is a matter of history and it is a matter of personal knowledge for the President that he knew precisely in 1969 she had proposed him as a Congress Candidate for election to the office of the President of India and her proposition was passed unanimously. However, she proceeded to work for and secured the success of an independent candidate, Mr. V.V. Giri, who was consequently elected as the President of India. . . if in the first instance it was Charan Singh's duty, before he spoke of unconditional support, to put it plainly to Mrs. Gandhi and her party that before giving their support it should be clearly understood that the special courts would not be abolished and the prosecution would not be withdrawn. If in pursuit of his life's ambition he failed to discharge that duty, it was clearly incumbent upon the President to put that question directly to Mrs. Gandhi and to Mr. Stephen when they met him. The statement put out after the Ministry was sworn in, namely that the unconditional obligation to support Ch. Charan Singh ended once he was sworn in, had they been mentioned to or elicited by the President would have made it clear that Ch.

Charan Singh did not have the unconditional support of the Congress (I) and could not form a stable government.

Charan Singh Resigns

It may be mentioned that the predictable thing happened and on the morning of 20th August, 1979 which had been fixed for vote of confidence in Ch. Charan Singh's Government, the Congress (I) headed by Smt. Indira Gandhi decided to oppose the motion. Ch. Charan Singh resigned and stated that there were more important things in life than being a Prime Minister and he could not be a party to a bargain by which the Special Courts would be abolished and the prosecution withdrawn. Had he put India first and life's ambition second he should have adopted this high moral tone before obtaining the support of Mrs. Gandhi's party. Coming as it did after he was driven from office by Mrs. Gandhi's party, his talk of moral principles was unreal.

The former Minister of External Affairs expressed the general feeling of people when he said "politicians have become a laughing stock. They have become worse than prostitutes. How can we show our face to the world?"

The events leading upto, and following the fall of Janata Government have led people to wonder whether conventions evolved in the United Kingdom can apply to the very difference conditions, prevailing in India.

The grave danger to our democratic constitution posed by defection and the means of averting that dangers are considered later. However, since the question whether the British conventions apply to the exercise of President's powers must be answered in the frame work of our constitution, it is beyond doubt that those conventions clearly apply.

The President's action was clearly contrary to Art. 75(3) and the convention which is necessarily implied in that Article. The President ought not to have called that person to form a Government unless he commanded the confidence of the majority of the House of the People. If the President considered that more time was required to secure that and more time should have been given to both the contestants before appointing any person as Prime Minister. Admittedly Ch. Charan Singh did not command a majority in the House of the People; consequently his having a large number of supporters than Mr. Desai was irrelevant. To have given him three week's time to find out whether he could secure the necessary majority was contrary to the Principle underlying Art. 75(1) and 75 (3) of the Constitution of India. The extreme importance of adhering to the Principle underlying Art. 75(1) and 75 (3) will be obvious, if the grave consequences of its breach are considered.

In any event, if the object of the President and of all the parties upto that time was to avoid mid-term poll, it was wrong for the President not to have called upon Jagjivan Ram to form an alternative government. The fact that the other parties to serve their own interest expressed themselves in favour of a mid-term poll, when nothing had changed except that the leader of the largest party expressed his readiness and ability to form a stable government could not absolve the President from his duty to put the interest of the country above the interest of a large number of fragmented and hostile parties. It has been suggested that for the President to have called upon Mr. Jagjivan Ram as the Leader of the Party of 205 Janata M.Ps. would have been to discourage defection. This suggestion can only be described as grotesque after President Reddy had called upon the great defector, Ch. Charan Singh, to form a government. As stated earlier, it is much easier for a party of 205 members to secure the necessary support in a House of 544 members than for a leader of about 75 members. It is submitted that the President's action was not only improper and discriminatory but led to a situation in which he should never have placed the country. He set up a government which never commanded the confidence of the House of the People at all; that government was to remain in power for a period of four months.

The President of India has thus presented to the world the humiliating spectacle of a great democratic country being ruled by a government which never commanded the confidence of the House of the People.

(In the case of Shri Inder Kumar Gujral, the situation was no better. While taking over as Prime Minister Mr. Gujral was neither a member of Lok Sabha, nor did he command the confidence of the majority of the House of the People).

The latest case of Smt. Sushma Swaraj is still the worst. Six weeks before the Assembly Elections to be held on 25th November, 1998, she replaced the duly elected Chief Minister—Sahib Singh Varma—and took over as Chief Minister without being a member of the Legislative Assembly. She brought a shame and embarrassment of the highest order for her party and the office of the Chief Minister by acting as a dictator in gross violation of the model code of conduct. She brought down the graph of BJP considerably and had been the main cause of the rout of the BJP in all the states where Assembly elections were held. We shall speak about her more in a separate chapter.

Era of Outside Support

Mushroom parties played havoc, and had been the main reason for the fall of the governments one after the other. And the outside support was nothing but an instrument of blackmailing by the political parties.

After Rajiv Gandhi, V.P. Singh became the Prime Minister with outside support by the BJP.

After the fall of V.P. Singh's government when the BJP withdrew its support, Chandra Shekhar was appointed as the next Prime Minister, with the outside support of the Congress headed by Shri Rajiv Gandhi.

The appointment of Deve Gowda, as the Prime Minister was nothing but a mockery of democracy. While withdrawing support from Deve Gowda Government Sita Ram Kesri, the then Congress President called him Nikamma (inefficient) on the floor of the House. Parliament debates will show the heaps of abuses showered on Deve Gowda at the time of No Confidence Debate in the Lok Sabha.

And the appointment of Shri. I.K. Gujral as Prime Minister immediately after the fall of Deve Gowda in which he himself was the External Affairs Minister, is nothing but a fraud on the constitution. He accepted the outside support of Congress, which called his own Prime Minister, Deve Gowda, a nikamma (inefficient).

Soon after becoming the Prime Minister Gujral also started getting threats of withdrawal of outside support by the Congress party as also the CPI (M).

Sita Ram Kesri even predicted the fall of Gujral Government any day. Not only this, the Congress President while addressing the congress workers conference at Patna openly said that the 13 party government headed by I.K. Gujral will not last longer. And I quote "I do not believe that this 13 party government will last" he told a Congress workers Conference here (Patna)." Statesman 10.9.1997.

"Don't take congress for granted Kesri tells United Front".

> "Congress President Sita Ram Kesri today expressed doubts about the longevity of the United Front and said coalition governments were not in the interest of the country. The United Front's 13 party government had inherent contradictions which made the task of its survival daunting."
>
> "He strongly defended his decision to withdraw support from H.D. Deve Gowda Ministry."
>
> *Economic Times 10.9.1997*
>
> In rebuttal, Prime Minister I.K. Gujral had said, "the coalition politics in the country has come to stay and that it had helped considerably in reducing tensions between the centre and the states."

Author's Views

That outside support is unknown to the constitution. The working of the govt. is based on the collective responsibility of the entire cabinet of Ministers headed by the Prime Minister.

Art. 75(3) of the Constitution clearly lays down that "the council of Ministers shall be collectively responsible to the House of People". The past experience of coalition governments and the outside support by the political parties have shown miserable results. The fall of Morarji Desai, Ch. Charan Singh, V.P. Singh, Chandra Shekhar, H.D. Deve Gowda governments are the living examples.

Writ petitions in the High Court and the Supreme Court

The appointment of Shri H.D. Deve Gowda as Prime Minister was challenged in the High Court and the Supreme Court of India but the points raised therein did not convince the judges to lay down the law on the validity of such type of appointments. The legislature can certainly bring suitable amendments in the Constitution preventing such type of coalition governments, and restraining the non-members to hold the office of Prime Minister.

A writ petition was also filed by this writer (Dr. Janak Raj Jai vs. Prime Minister of India and another—C.W. P. No. 1861/97 in the High Court of Delhi) challenging the validity of outside support to Gujral Government. But before the court could decide the matter on merits, the Gujral Government had already fallen. So the said writ petition became infructuous.

The Latest Coalition Government

Inspite of our appeal in the earlier book—'Voter's Dilemma' for a single party rule, the voters chose not to give a clear mandate in the 12th Lok Sabha Election. The result is, Shri Atal Behari Vajpayee has to run the government with the support of 18 parties. We shall be discussing the plight of Vajpayee government in a different chapter.

S.R. Bommai, former President of Janata Dal, and a Union Cabinet Minister expressed his views publically that to run the governments by outside support, or to have a coalition government is not at all a healthy practice.

P.A. Sangma, a former Lok Sabha Speaker strongly felt that the status of the Prime Minister was under considerable strain in coalition government because of pressure from comparatively smaller coalition partners. He further said that "the Chief Ministers are driven to function less autonomously than under single party rule because of pressure even from comparatively smaller constituents."

Recounting his experience as head of an eight-party coalition government in the north-eastern state, Mr. Sangma said "every single moment was a moment of black-mailing".

He said that the interest in a coalition at the centre could be inconsistent with its interest in the state, leading to conflict of interests between national level leadership of the party and the state level party functionaries.

Mr. Sangma further said that the Prime Minister must belong to Lok Sabha and not the upper house as was in the case of I.K. Gujral or his predecessor H.D. Deve Gowda.

> "It is my personal opinion and considered view that the Prime Minister must belong to the House of People, that is what Parliamentary Democracy is all about. Mr. Sangma said in response to a question about the "disturbing trend of Prime Ministers preferring the Rajya Sabha. "(The Times of India—23.8.1997.)

In a recent statement, Rajesh Pilot, a senior CWC Member, said in so many words that days of coalition governments would soon be over. The coalition governments have done precious little towards the welfare and betterment of the people. And the need of the hour, therefore, is that there must be one party rule at the centre to strengthen the democratic functioning at all levels.

The Statesman of 27th December, 1998 carries an Editorial, under the caption "One party Logic (Avoid Coalitions and Keep your virtues)". The same is approvingly reproduced below:

One Party Logic—Avoid Coalitions and Keep your Virtue

One reason why the general perception about the Congress has improved is that Sonia Gandhi is still viewed as a non-political person, even though she is Congress President and has fought an election as such. This says something about the general powers of perception of the political class as a whole. There is Bofors, certainly, but despite this Sonia Gandhi is not generally seen to be indulging in base politics, entering into shady political contracts for short-term benefits, or consorting with the corrupt and the greedy. That is basically because she stands outside coalition politics and is thus spared the compromises and the political precariousness that goes with it. Besides which, she provides the Congress Party with a symbolic link with its monolithic past by virtue of the family she married into. Nobody can say what the future has in store, given the fact that the electorate continues to be fragmented and that a certain amount of flux is to be expected. But the logic dictated by the need to maintain the integrity of leadership and a style that is aiming at a high degree of commitment to policies, is a one-party logic. Sonia Gandhi's leadership style is one that banks rather heavily on prestige and on leaders and, therefore, to see her involved in petty deal-making or held hostage by the likes of Mulayam Singh Yadav and Laloo Prasad Yadav, will be extremely damaging to her aura or charisma she cultivates so assiduously. It is correct to say that the Congress party and its President are hoping for some kind of general disillusionment with coalition politics and resurgence of the desire for a more stable political situation where the man in charge knows exactly what is going on.

Besides which, there are other features of this political style which need to be noted. For instance, it is very low on rhetoric. That is because Sonia Gandhi, despite having fought an election, is not in a position where she can address the masses on a regular basis. Many will say it is her Italianness that comes in the way of indulging in rhetorical flamboyance that is usually associated with political leadership in this country. That may be true; for one who speaks Hindi as, more or less, a foreign tongue, it is not easy to be spontaneous and biting at the same time. But, on the other hand, this can also constitute an advantage to the extent that it conveys an impression of sobriety and dignity, whether true or false is a different matter. However, the one-party logic will not be easy to translate into reality. One victory in Agra East does not mean much for, as SP secretary Amar Singh points, the party had no presence there, it was a BJP bastion. In Bihar, the RJD managed to win all four by-elections and even though the Bihar unit of the party was clamouring to go it alone, the state is not there for the taking. Ultimately and curiously, even though the SP chief has already declared the Congress to be enemy number one, it may be on BJP territory that the Congress will have to do much of its poaching in the future; it is unlikely that the SP, RJD and BSP constituencies in UP and Bihar will be wiped out overnight or succumb to some wave. So, it is crucial for the Congress both to keep its distance from the social justice parties and to wait for the BJP to succumb the pressures of its own realpolitik. What all this proves is that regional and caste-based equations are almost impossible to manage from the perspective of a party which aspires to govern at the Centre, a lesson that the BJP is trying to learn."

VINASH KALE VIPREET BUDDHI

There is a popular saying that when bad days come, the wisdom goes on a long holiday. The BJP leadership's decision to project Smt. Sushma Swaraj as the next Chief Minister of the National Capital Territory of Delhi sealed the future of BJP in Delhi in particular, and in other states in general for at least one decade, or so. 12th of October, 1998, will go down as the darkest day in the history of the Bharatiya Janata Party, when its leadership decided to replace Shri Sahib Singh Verma, the sitting Chief Minister, with the so called pretty lady Sushma Swaraj in gross violation of the Constitution of India, Model Code of Conduct and the well settled conventions under a democratic set up.

There was lot of resentment among the top local leadership, on her dramatic appointment as the Chief Minister of Delhi, replacing the duly elected Chief Minister, in a very shameful and disgraceful manner. All the MLAs were summoned at the party headquarters and were forced to vote in favour of Sushma Swaraj as the next Chief Minister. There was a silent dissent in the BJP circles, as no one from the local leadership could reconcile on the appointment of an outsider as the Chief Minister of Delhi.

Reacting to the appointment of Shrimati Sushma Swaraj as the Chief Minister, Statesman of 19th October, 1998 published a letter to the Editor from one enlightened citizen—S.K. Shah, which gives a very interesting reading. To quote: this is apropos of Editorial "Just a pretty face" (13th October). At last the BJP mandarins showed Mr. Sahib Singh Verma the door merely six weeks before the Delhi Assembly elections were due, whenever a change of guard takes place, more often than not, ridiculous explanations are offered, justifying such a change. It is in this context, that BJP General Secretary Mr. Venkaiah Naidu's statement—that it had nothing to do with any panic reaction over the dismal performance of Mr. Verma leading to his departure—will amuse none.

Delhi's residents have been crying hoarse over complete breakdown of services like, power, water, transport, the inconvenience arising out of strikes by doctors, and nurses and now spiralling prices. This year's summer has been the most worst in living memory; Delhiites continued to suffer even as ex-C.M., in a pre election frenzy, launched and announced populist schemes. The BJP high command dithered over taking a decision to replace Mr. Sahib Singh. The citizens meanwhile kept on suffering.

Politics is the art of survival. The agony of Delhiites failed to move the BJP leaders to act, but the seemingly imminent rout at the hustings forced them to foist Mrs. Sushma Swaraj who has a political base in Haryana, as the Delhi Chief Minister. Management of mundane problems of a vast and complex city like Delhi requires more than just communication skills. Ms. Swaraj is connoisseur of this Art.

The change was made only when the BJP found its boat sinking and not as consequence of the people's problems. The realisation that the Delhiites cup of woe is full did not dawn upon the top BJP brass from public outcry. Political expediency made them work.

Expecting Mrs. Swaraj to tilt the electoral fortunes in favour of BJP is a wishful thinking, more so when the faction ridden party with Jat and Punjabi lobbies represented by Mr. Sahib Singh Verma and Khurana, Malhotra—Sahni group are licking their psychological wounds and the public having no respite from an apathetic government that remained in inertia for far too long.

Revolt in Local Leadership

Terming his removal from the Chief Ministership as an internal matter of the party, Mr. Singh admitted that the manner in which the entire thing had been carried out did not go too well with the people of Delhi. The Jats of Delhi held mahapanchayats in Delhi condemning the high command in removing Sahib Singh Verma, and even they came out with threats that they would not work for the BJP in the assembly elections. This statement did have a bad effect in all the states where the assembly elections were being held on the same day i.e. 25.11.1998.

On the dropping of Ranjindra Gupta from her cabinet, Sushma Swaraj earned the wrath of Vaishya community in the capital in particular, and in other states in general.

The Punjabi lobby in Delhi also came out openly against the appointment of Smt. Sushma Swaraj as the Chief Minister of Delhi. Addressing the press conference, Rashtriya Punjabi Mahasangh Chairman Hardyal Devgun said, "The appointment of Mr. Khurana as the Chief Minister at this stage would have benefited the party as he has better organising capacity than other party leaders."

Mr. Devgun stated that the move to promote Mr. Sahib Singh to the cabinet could have been welcomed, if Mr. Khurana had simultaneously been made the Chief Minister of Delhi. Mr. Khurana has been ignored because he is a Punjabi, and anti Punjabi lobby has succeeded to marganilise the Punjabi leadership", he said.

The former MP claimed that they were only trying to highlight the feelings of the Punjabi community in Delhi and trying to bring it out before the BJP leadership. Mr. Devgun said as of now, "they would continue to back the BJP. . . ."

Mr. Devgun who worked as Mr. Khurana's election agent in the Lok Sabha election, said that, "Mr. Khurana and the Punjabi community had been the back-bone of the Jan Sangh and then the BJP in Delhi."

The former MP from East Delhi said it was unfortunate that "the BJP and the RSS, which were working for Hindu consolidation too had given into pressures of casteist politics."

"The holding of Panchayats by one community, airing the grievances at a press conference, and branding Mrs. Sushma Swaraj as Brahmin leader, and brandishing unbecoming threats to all and sundry including Punjabis do not go well with the ideology of national unity and Hindu consolidation for which the BJP and the RSS are known" Mr. Devgun said.

Mr. Devgun claimed that the Punjabi community had been voting for the BJP for the last three decades "but it was painful for them that their leaders were being sidelined". He referred to the manner in which former Delhi BJP President Kidarnath Sahni, was sidelined and the claims of Mr. Khurana for a second term in office were over-looked."

"While Mr. Khurana should have been the ideal person to ensure a victory for the party, we now want an honourable settlement for Mr. Khurana. He should be gracefully involved in the affairs of the Delhi Unit" he said. The Punjabi leaders issued an appeal to former Chief Minister, Sahib Singh Verma to restrain his supporters from indulging in caste politics.

Transgressing the Jurisdiction

Overnight, Sushma Swaraj transforms herself from information and broadcasting into the Chief Minister of Delhi, with a definite agenda to win. "We will definitely win", she beams, adding that it was a calculated decision by her senior colleagues to place her, where she finds herself now. She takes upon herself the task of visiting the police stations admonishing the police officers for not doing their duty properly, knowing fully well that the police is not under the state, it is under the centre. Even the Chief Election Commissioner reprimanded her for violating the Code of Conduct by transgressing her jurisdiction, in order to influence and gain sympathy from the voters of Delhi.

"And she has drawn blood. The SHO of Kalyanpuri was literally caught with his pants down, the other day, when the Chief Minister went calling on him. She was after all keeping her promise of not sleeping till the entire city slept well, not fitfully."

Taking leaf out of the stories on benevolent kings of Yore, who travelled, disguised to take stock of the law and order in their kingdom, the newly crowned Chief Minister, soon after taking charge travelled incognito in a private car, hoping to take errant cops unaware. And she succeeded, when she swooped down on the unsuspecting policemen in the East Delhi Police Station (chosen mainly for its ever rising crime graph), she found the SHO missing from his seat. Determined to talk to him, she waited for two hours before she decided to summon the senior police officers.

If the SHO had been caught napping, it perhaps would not have merited more than a rap on the knuckles. Since he had vamoosed (perhaps even drunk) in his kuchha banyan, the Minister hit the roof. The errant officer was immediately suspended and the furious Chief Minister had already written a note to the Home Minister for further action.

Yet, clearly the entire SHO incident has left her amused, alarmed, and a little shaken . . . comfortably ensconced in a huge Swivel Chair just vacated by her reluctant predecessor, Sahib Singh Verma, she regales her attendants and media persons with the amusing story of the kuchcha banyan clad SHO. "He must have been drunk while on duty and did not want to see me clad in his underpants. If the SHO of a crime infested place like Kalyanpuri shirks work, I shudder to think the state of law in the capital" says Swaraj . . . Seven bleary eyed cabinet colleagues prowling the streets of Delhi in the fond hope that sleepless citizens reeling under the threat of dropsy, bludgeoned, by the deteriorating law and order situation, spiralling onion prices, collapsing law and order situation, can sleep. Thus narrates Anuradha Raman in Pioneer of 18th October, 1998.

Singing Songs in her Own Praise

Soon after taking over as the Chief Minister of Delhi the glamorous lady started singing songs in her own praise. And in her over enthusiasm Sushma Swaraj claimed that a change of face would substantially brighten the chances of her party. She also admitted that Delhiites were disillusioned with the BJP government during the past six months. Describing herself as the 'Universally acceptable face' for the Chair of the Chief Minister, she admitted in unequivocal terms that the people were angry with the BJP because of the accumulated effect of power and water cuts last summer, dropsy deaths, deteriorating law and order situation and spiralling prices of onions, forgetting this fact that she herself was at the centre, as also the fact that there is a BJP led government, at the centre, she openly blamed the BJP led Central Government for deteriorating law and order situation.

'Face the Media Programme' at Press Club of India

The Statesman of 23rd October, 1998 carries a detailed story of Shrimati Sushma Swaraj's interview at a "Face the media' programme organised by the Press Club of India. The same is reproduced below:

"BJP strategy for M.P., Mizoram, and Rajasthan Polls."

Candidates for CM to be projected.

The BJP will project its chief ministerial candidates for next month's assembly elections in Madhya Pradesh, Rajasthan and Mizoram, the Delhi Chief Minister, Mrs. Sushma Swaraj said here today.

Having reviewed the political situation, the party decided to project the candidates for chief ministership. You will see projection of the Chief Ministers in all the four states, after the party's next meeting. "Mrs. Swaraj said, asserting that she was brought in Delhi as the party thought a change of face would substantially brighten our chances."

She was replying to queries by reporters at a 'face the media' programme organised at the Press Club of India here today. During the question answer session, Mrs. Swaraj admitted that Delhiites were disillusioned with the BJP government during the past six months. Asked whether her projection as Chief Minister would deny new legislators the right to choose their leader, she said 'The process of consultations with legislators was not bypassed. Prior and post poll consultations take place."

"We are in a parliamentary democracy in which political parties have a significant role and are more important than individuals', she said, adding that consultations did take place, 'only the timing is different."

On her reluctance to take over as the Chief Minister initially Mrs. Swaraj said she did not want to replace her colleague, Mr. Sahib Singh. And in an apparent dig at Mr. Madan Lal Khurana who had expressed his displeasure at her taking over, she added, 'it does not befit anyone to go after a post after replacing a colleague.

The Chief Minister, however, made it clear that she was neither 'out of the national scene for good', nor was her exit from the Union Cabinet due to resentment among some ministers over her style of functioning. Replying to a query, Mrs. Swaraj said it was a common practice for Union Ministers to become Chief Minister and vice versa. **Mrs. Swaraj said there was substantial difference in her style of functioning than her predecessor, Mr. Sahib Singh, which was perceptible.** To make the point, she later referred to her government's request to the Centre to put onions in the list of items under the open general licence which was immediately agreed to. The Centre's committee on pricing had put onion in the list the next day on a Food Ministry's proposal.

The Chief Minister said no one expected a miracle in her month long tenure to solve all the problems in Delhi, specially since she not only did not have much time, but had her hands tied due to the election code of conduct. **'I can only give a glimpse of a better Delhi and instill confidence that things would look up better', she said,**

Mrs. Swaraj—who described herself as the 'universally acceptable face' for the Chief Minister's chair admitted that people were angry with the BJP because of the accumulated effect of power and water cuts last summer, dropsy deaths, deteriorating law and order situation and spiralling prices of onions.

She however, emphasised that though people were disillusioned with the government during the past six months, it was clear that they have recognised the government's achievements during the remaining four and a half years since the BJP's poll percentage had increased during the three elections, two Lok Sabha elections and one for the Municipal Corporation—held after the BJP came to power in 1993.

Mrs. Swaraj said she would remind the people of the achievements of the government during this period which they had forgotten. We are proud of our past performance, she said, adding that the party was neither apologetic nor ashamed of its performance.

The Chief Minister also pointed out that the Delhi Government could not be blamed for the onion crisis and the deteriorating law and order situation since these came under the purview of the Centre. The Centre, she said, had allowed export of onions till August since it could not have expected to anticipate the crop failure due to extended rains.

Alleged Scandals in the Purchase of Onions

In an independent Chapter, "Sushma and her Onions", we have tried to bring out detailed stories on 'the onion muddle', which needs a thorough probe for the information of the people at large, who suffered in silence helplessly and haplessly. And even during the Four Day Assembly Session, when the new government took over, there was a heated debate demanding a full probe on the onion purchases.

Onion Sold in Black Market

The BJP MLA, Prof. P.K. Chandla, in his statement as appeared in Hindi Hindustan dated 30.10.1998, said that the onions which were to be sold at subsidised rates, were sold in black market. "The onions which are meant for the general public, are being distributed among the selected privileged persons," he further said.

Importing Onions not a Violation of EC Code*

The Chief Minister, Mrs. Sushma Swaraj, today said the Delhi Government's decision to airlift onions from Iran to meet its acute shortage, was not a violation of the election code of conduct.

"The government is within its right to import the commodity to meet the needs of its citizens", she said at a Press conference here today, adding only "populist announcements" fell within the ambit of the model code of conduct.

She said the daily onion requirement of the Capital was around 400 tonnes which the government would be able to meet with the imports. Mrs. Swaraj said the government would also look at the possibility of importing onion from other countries where onions are available at competitive rates.

Mrs. Swaraj had announced on Sunday that the government would airlift onions from Iran to tide over its sudden shortage due to rains in Nasik, from where it was being supplied to the Capital.

---

* Statesman News Service, New Delhi, Oct. 20.

She denied the allegation of discrimination against a particular community by not including the former Transport Minister, Mr. Rajendra Gupta, in her cabinet, saying that her party had never believed in 'casteism". Upon asking why the BJP had changed its earlier stand of not projecting any leader for the Chief Ministership prior to the Assembly elections in her case, she said every political party had a right to review its election strategy at an appropriate time.

Mrs. Swaraj said she had issued instructions to Delhi Vidyut Board officials to ensure that its complaint centres were manned at all times. The Chief Minister said they had also been told that the officials were also directed to ensure that all complaints were redressed as early as possible. "you will find a change in their working in a few days," she said, indicating that their functioning so far had not been to her satisfaction. Mrs. Swaraj also said the DVB officials had been told to complete processing of applications for power connections to people residing in unauthorised colonies which had paid the requisite charges."

SUSHMA AND THE ONION CRISIS

Here are sensational exposures in the onion mess-up, muddle and bungling

Legal Notice

New Delhi Dated November 17th 1998
Delhi State Civil Supplies Corporation Ltd.
Through Sh. R.B. Sehgal
Company Secretary,
Aapurti Bhawan, 7–9, Aram Bagh,
Pahar Ganj, New Delhi.

Chief Minister's Office.
Old Secretariat, Delhi.

Dear Sirs,

Under Instructions from and on behalf of our client M/S. MSM Trading Est. Dubai, we serve upon you the following legal notice.

1. That this is in reference to contract document dated 9-10-98 between Delhi State Civil Supplies Corporation Ltd., Delhi through its company secretary Shri R.B. Sehgal and our client MSM Trading Est. through Shri Arun Bhan for the supply of 3000 MTS of grade A Onions of Iranian origin.
2. That according to the terms of the contract referred herein, your addressee No. 1 was bound to open an Irrevocable and transferable internationally acceptable Letter Of Credit, as per the International standards on the 10th October, 1998 early morning.
3. That for sincerely operating the contract and to supply the required quantity and quality, it was imperative to

have the Letter of Credit opened on 10.10.1998 early morning. But because of your callous attitude, you deliberately delayed the same by three days making the contract not a valid document, as time was the essence of the contract.

4. Your Act of Omission and Commission shows that you are totally inexperienced regarding the International standards of Trade of Imports & Exports, and you never took the contract seriously under some deliberate pressures.
5. That it appears from the subsequent events that some political pressure was built against our client in regard to the transaction entered into with our client, in as much as from the office of your Addressee No. 2 (who was never in picture till then) summoning our client to renegotiate the rates of supplies of Onions as per the above referred contract entered accordingly upon which, only the non negotiable clauses under the letter of Credit were to be made operational and negotiable and when my client refused to come to Delhi and renegotiate the rates, bureaucratic hurdles were put into it making the contract almost inoperative.
6. That with a view to avoid your obligations/liabilities under the contract, you dishonestly and with malafide intentions, opened a non-working, non-acceptable and non-negotiable Letter of Credit, with the result that entire transaction fizzled out to the total disadvantage of our client. It was not even appreciated that in case of the normal local cheque, it takes atleast two to three full working days to get the payment of the cheque well within the same city but in our client's case, absolutely ineffective time of just two working days were given (As out of four days, two days were holidays on account of Sunday and Diwali). It is simply imprudent and devoid of common sense to provide just two days in the letter of Credit while a minimum of 15 to 20 days are provided under the International laws of trading for the purpose of Imports & Exports for multiparty and multi country Letter of Credit. (As it involved five parties in three countries for this transaction.)
7. That you intentionally avoided the fulfillment of the Contract for the reasons best known to you but your conduct

has made our client to suffer heavy losses on account of his onwards commitments. Our client communicated various letters to you in this regard. However you stopped all communications with my client and within the continuation of my clients contract, entered into a contract with another party for the supply of onions almost three times the rates finalized with us, the reasons of which are best known to you.

8. That in order to honestly fulfill the commitment in the above mentioned contract our client incurred the actual expenses on travelling from Delhi-Bombay-Dubai and back twice long conversations on telephone, on mobile telephone and by sending long letters by way of fax to fulfil the contractual obligations, to the tune of INR 3,00,000/-

   Our client was also put under heavy losses because of the amount given as advance for the shipment of 800 MT of Onions for 15th and 1000MT of Onions for 16th to the tune of US $ 59,400 amounting to approx. INR 25 lakh. Not only this, a sum of approx. US $ 8,000 (INR 3.5 lakh) were also spent for Vessel/container booking.

9. Our client has also lost profits @ 20% of the total value of the contract value. Besides above amounts, our clients suffered mental tension, anxiety, worry, physical inconvenience in running up and down from pillar to post to ensure timely supply of Onions. Our client quantifies the damages on this account for a sum of INR 2,50,000/-.

We, therefore, call upon you all to pay the above amounts referred in paragraph 7,8 & 9 along with a sum of INR 11,000/- as charges of this notice severally or jointly within 7 days of receipt of this notice, failing which we have very clear instructions to initiate legal proceedings at all levels to expose you and also for the recovery of amount and such other relief that our client is entitled to against you all completely and our risks as to cost and consequences.

A copy of this notice is kept in our office for reference and record.

Narendra Kalra
Advocate

Onion Import: Dubai-based Firm Slaps Legal Notice on BJP Government*

A firm entrusted with import of Iranian onion in October has served a legal notice on the Delhi State Civil Supplies Corporation (DSCSC) and the Delhi Government through the Chief Minister's office for failing to fulfil the terms of the contract in time due to which onions could not reach Delhi in time.

The MSM Trading Est, Dubai, shot off the legal notice yesterday alleging that the Delhi Government had failed to open an irrevocable and internationally transferable and acceptable Letter of Credit in the favour of the firm on the due date for import of onion. Despite repeated attempts, the DSCSC could not be contacted for their version of the episode. An official spokesperson for the Delhi Government said he was unaware of whether the legal notice had been served or not.

Interestingly, the MSM Trading Est had agreed to supply 3,000 Metric Tonnes (MTS) of onion for Rs. 3.16 crores but the Delhi Government settled for 750 MTS of onion which another firm agreed to supply for Rs. 3.36 crore.

Accordingly to the legal notice issued by Mr. Narender Kalra, MSM's legal representative in India, the Delhi Government has handled the whole deal in a callous fashion under 'deliberate pressure'. "Your act of omission and commission shows that you are totally inexperienced regarding the international standards of Trade of Imports and Exports and you never took the contract seriously under some deliberate pressure." the notice read.

The MSM Trading Est signed a contract with the Delhi Government on Oct. 9, three days before Ms. Sushma Swaraj took over as the Chief Minister, for supply of 3,000 MTS of onion. The consignment was to reach in phases by ship at Mumbai port by Oct. 19.

The firm alleges malafide intentions behind not opening the LC in time due to which the consignment could not reach Delhi. The Delhi Government later agreed to import lesser quantity of onions at a higher rate.

---

* By Poornima Joshi, *The Hindustan Times* 21.11.98, New Delhi, November 20.

BJP Clutches at Straws, Subsidises Swadeshi Onions*

The Sushma Swaraj-led BJP made a desperate bid to reclaim lost ground in the past one week. The Party's star campaigner and PM Atal Behari Vajpayee chipped in with six election meetings and Home Minister L.K. Advani addressed eight. The entire party machinery was galvanised. But there was something else taking place on the sly.

Like any other party in power, the BJP too pulled a fast one. The onion price hike issue was fast outstripping all its efforts to mobilise public opinion in its favour. The government pumped in Rs. 12 crore to subsidise the price of swadeshi onions. Close to another Rs. 10 crore was spent on importing onions. To woo voters in some select unauthorised colonies, the BJP government also released Rs. 20 crore at one go for their development. None of this was publicised. No press release was issued.

The reason: the EC may be watching. But the tell-tale signs were all there. The BJP government bought onion for Rs. 30 a kg. only to sell it for Rs. 10 a kg. Last week the outlets selling subsidised onion were increased many times. The Azadpur wholesalers-turned-retailers were selling vegetables almost on a no-profit, no-loss basis, thanks to the government subsidy which is actually the tax-payers' money.

Food and Civil Supplies secretary K. Sethuraman confirmed that Rs. 12 crore was spent to subsidise the pricely onion. The money was released in four installments since mid-October. The first installment was of Rs. 1 crore, the second Rs. 1.5 crore and the third Rs. 3 crore. The Delhi Government was asked to release Rs. 6.5 crore as the fourth installment just last week.

Sethuraman clarified that the Central Government had already been paying for the subsidy since July this year. But he admits that the state government decided to contribute its mite on September 26. Significantly, the largest chunk of this subsidy came only this month. Similarly, the BJP government decided to rope in voters residing in unauthorised colonies when it released Rs. 20 crore to the MCD to carry out devel-

* By Raman Kirpal, New Delhi, November 24.

opment activities, like constructing nullahs and sewerage facilities, took place only this month.

During the Annual Plan, beginning April 1998, the government had allocated Rs. 41 crore under 'Unauthorised Colonies'. But till September, not a paisa had been released from the fund.

When the elections were announced, the government woke up and released the sum at one go. How and where the money was spent will only be determined when the MCD submits the utilisation certificate? Between onion and unauthorised colonies, the Delhi government blew up Rs. 32 crore.

Import of Onions by Delhi Government Swaraj & Pyaaj—Few Relevant Questions

1. Why was the opening of the electronic letter of credit delayed for more than 4 days despite the sense of urgency and panic prevailing in the NCT of Delhi over the Onions issue? Does it not reflect the inherent contradictions prevailing in the BJP leadership wherein the decisions taken by the predecessor are viewed suspiciously by the follower?
2. What caused the occurrence of such basic and fundamental defects in the letter of credit, and why was it not made internationally acceptable by removing these basic defects? Could the occurrence of such basic errors from such high/professional authorities be attributed to ignorance of international norms?
3. Why did the new CM recommend onions to be put under OGL? Was it not a rash step to promote hoarding rather than serving any constructive purpose?
4. Who is Mr. Satish Gupta? Why and under whose instructions did he call up Dubai?
5. What prompted Mr. Satish Gupta to remark that the already contracted prices were too high and the matter needed to be "negotiated" at Delhi? Does this not reflect the malafide intentions of certain vested interests?
6. Why the CM did not come on line when called? Why she did not call back the party despite specific message for the same? Why the party was told to contact Satish Gupta

at that time? And how else, could the party have contacted the CM, other than on her regular and mobile numbers?

7. Why was DSCSC Ltd. so insensitive to the entire transaction and what prompted the organization to stop communicating with MSM after 15.10.98?
8. What justifies the import of onions @ Rs. 30/- Kg through this private party whereas the supplies could have easily reached @ Rs. 10.71/- Kg by the 21st of October 98 had the L/C been made internationally acceptable? Was any tender thrown for the purchase or the CM acted on her own?
9. What is the proximity of CM/her husband Shri Swaraj Kaushal with this private party?
10. Why couldn't this private party supply the contracted quantity at such an exorbitant price of Rs. 30 also? What action was taken against that party?
11. Why was a step motherly treatment meted out to other states by giving a subsidy to the Delhi Govt. only? Was Delhi the only state caught in the web of rising prices of onions?
12. What is the status of the Rs. 10 Crore subsidies given by the Central Govt.? Was this subsidy meant to remove the scarcity of onions or was it the price for creating a general type by airlifting small quantities of onions? Under the circumstances, don't you think it has been grossly misutilised?
13. Since when did DSCSC Ltd. start operating on Sundays? What caused so much of panic in the organization that a show cause notice was faxed to MSM on a Sunday by an organization that had turned completely deaf and dumb to the entire transaction even on normal working days for good 10 days?
14. Why the Government got panicky and gave a hurried advertisement in Pioneer on 25.10.98? Why they did not advertise on 16/17th before giving the contract to private party rather than on 25.10.98?
15. Where did the MSM files disappear when the Indian Export tried to probe the matter? Were the following reactions mere co-incidences:

The CM deliberately avoided discussion on the matter.

The State Food Minister Ms. Poornima Sethi remarked that she was too busy supervising the flood situation and so she was completely unaware of the transaction of onions of her own ministry?

The DSCSC Ltd. Chairman was evasive on the issue and she directed to talk to the MD for any details.

Incidentally the MD by that time was on a 'long leave'.

The Sr. G.M. knew nothing about the matter.

And the irony is that DSCSC Ltd. has provided mobile phones at the cost of Government of India with international connections to all its employees mentioned above, yet none was available on any of the phones: home, office or mobile.

16. The CM was over enthusiastic about the onions issue when she joined in. And after this controversy erupted, she just disappeared and stopped communicating on the matter. Why?
17. Why are the Prime Minister, Home Minister, Lt. Governor and other senior officials tight lipped on the matter? None of them has bothered to respond despite being updated with the actual position of onions import through MSM on 28th/29th last month itself?
18. What does the Delhi Government have to say about NAFED's offer to supply 2000 MTs of onions @ Rs. 8/- a Kg? Can this price of Rs. 8/Kg is any way being justified against a price of Rs. 30/Kg? Between 6th November, 1998 and 20th November, 1998, Delhi Government could have saved crores of rupees, had they purchased onions from NAFED at Rs. 8/- a Kg instead they are purchasing from open market at 22/- to 27/- a Kg Why?
19. Does the CM has any moral right to stay in power, after all this episode? And who has lost in the whole process? She, the BJP, the Dubai based party or the country at large?

Collective Amnesia Over Onion 'Deal'*

The Delhi Government has struck a deal with a "private party" to import 750 tonne of onion from Iran, but who is it? A senior official said it is a Delhi-based export-import firm represented by "some Sawhney or Sahani".

But Food and Civil Supplies Minister Poornima Sethi said she has no idea; Chief Minister Sushma Swaraj is reluctant to elaborate; and the bureaucrats who probably okayed the deal can't recollect the name.

Sources said the firm which has offices in Iran was chosen because onion has been placed under the Open General License (OGL) category, allowing anyone to import the vegetable.

Express Newsline queries in the past two days, nevertheless, revealed that the choice of the "private party" was left to the discretion of "a couple of persons".

And five days after Chief Minister Sushma Swaraj announced her decision to import Iranian onion, most of the bureaucrats are still vague about the details.

The government is buying the onion through the Delhi State Civil Supplies Corporation which is headed by Krishnalekha Sood. But even Sood can't "remember" the name of the firm. "I think it is based in Iran, and has offices in Delhi," he said.

The minister said the government invited bids from several firms and this "private party" quoted the lowest rate (Rs. 30), while the rest asked for Rs. 40 per Kg. "Why don't you ask my MD," she said. The MD could not be contacted despite repeated attempts.

Poornima Sethi's position on the issue is, however, most surprising because onion is the hottest issue in her ministry. "I am standing in knee-deep water in Okhla now," she said over her cellphone last night. "In fact, I have been so busy with flood relief work over the past two days that I haven't had time to update myself on the onion front."

---

* *Express News Service*, New Delhi, October 22.

Today, she said 16.5 tonne of onion has reached IGI airport, and another 40 tonne is expected late in the evening. But she still does not know the identity of the firm.

Neither is she sure whether the Delhi Government will be buying the consignment at Rs. 30 per Kg. "It could be a little more or even less, I should be able to give you more details tomorrow," she said.

Chief Minister Sushma Swaraj, on the other hand, today announced that 50 tonne of Iranian onion reached Delhi yesterday. And by tomorrow 400 tonne of the 750-tonne consignment would be deposited in government godowns.

The Delhi Government is buying the consignment at Rs. 30 per Kg, and will sell it at Rs. 10 through subsidies counters, she said.

Onion Import: CM Scales Down Promise*

The Delhi Government has scaled down its ambitious plan to airlift 400 tonne of Iranian onion daily. Instead, it has struck a deal with a Delhi-based "private party" to import only 750 tonne by air in small consignments spread over the week.

The first part of the package, a 50 tonne consignment, is expected to reach IGI airport late this evening. Another 150 tonne is scheduled to reach tomorrow and the remaining in similar consignments subsequently. Additional consignments, "if required", will be brought by ship.

At Rs. 30 per Kg, the government will have to pay Rs. 2.25 crore to the "private party" for the 750-tonne consignment. And the subsidy—at Rs. 10 per Kg in Delhi—will cost the Government Rs. 75 lakh.

The Government has also decided to replace the 70 mobile vans selling subsidised onion in each of Delhi's assembly segments with permanent outlets. These outlets will be manned by Delhi State Civil Supplies Corporation officials and the sales will be overseen by the area SDMs. The quota for Mother Diary outlets will also be increased.

---

* *Express News Service*, New Delhi, October 21.

Steep air freight charges have apparently nudged Delhi Chief Minister Sushma Swaraj to rethink her announcement on Sunday that 400 tonne of onion would be airlifted daily from Iran starting today.

Swaraj, however, told Express Newsline that she changed her mind because onion consignments of the new crop from Nasik, Rajasthan and Gujarat have started to arrive at Azadpur. And NAFED has promised to increase its daily quota for Delhi from 44 tonne to 250 tonne. "This should ease the crisis," she said, "along with the 750-tonne package. But if required we will import more onion, which will be brought by ship."

She explained that the understanding with the "private party (which also has offices in Iran) is that they will take care of the freight charges and customs duty after procuring the vegetable at Rs. 10–12 in Iran. The vegetable will be ferried on Air Iran cargo aircraft, because Air-India does not operate any cargo flights between Iran and India. The Delhi Government-run Delhi State Civil Supplies Corporation will buy the total consignment at Rs. 30 per Kg (inclusive of all the charges) only after it reaches IGI airport. This consignment will then be available to Delhiites for Rs. 10 per Kg at the subsidised counters.

"Even in Azadpur we were buying onion for Rs. 32 per Kg. Since the Centre has decided to bring onion under the Open General Licence (OGL) category, it is now easier to import onion at lower prices," said Swaraj. Delhi Food and Civil Supplies Minister Poornima Sethi was, however, oblivious of the course of events on the onion front today. "I have been very busy in Okhla for the past two days with flood relief work. I couldn't even attend today's meeting in this regard," said Sethi.

Yet she was confident that importing Iranian onion (at Rs. 30 per Kg) works out to be cheaper than buying from NAFED which was quoting Rs. 18–20 per kg for Delhi's requirements.

"We are now looking into the possibility of importing more onion from Turkemenistan. The vegetable is available there at only Rs. 4 per Kg," said Sethi.

Government Pvt. Firm Trade Charges Over Onion Deal*

Delhi Chief Minister Sushma Swaraj had announced on October 21 that 750 tonne of onion would be imported from Iran within four days; six days later only 66.7 tonne of Iranian onion has landed at IGI airport:

"The deal has proved to be costly in more ways than one. It's costing the Government almost 500 Dollars more per tonne than it would have if the onion was brought by ship," says a senior official, "and it hasn't benefited Delhiites."

Moreover, another firm had agreed to import 3,000 tonne by ship for Rs. 3.21 crore earlier this month. This deal fell through.

Compare this with 750 tonne of the airlifted onion which costs Rs. 2.25 crore as well 1,000 tonne for Rs. 1.11 crore which a third firm will import by ship in November.

So the arithmetic is: The Government could have got 3,000 tonne for Rs. 3.21 crore; It will now get 1,750 tonne for Rs. 3.36 crore.

On October 9—three days before Swaraj took ove as Chief Minister—the Delhi State Civil Supplies Corporation (DSCSC) entered into an agreement with MSM Trading Est, Dubai to import 3,000 tonne of onion at 255 Dollars per tonne (Rs. 10.71 per kg). And the total consignment was to be unloaded in phases at Mumbai port by October 19.

But the deal never materialised. The Government says MSM Trading Est backed out and a showcause notice has been issued to the latter; the firm claims the Government's Letter of Credit was riddled with technical flaws, there was no question of backing out.

While MSM representatives insist that if they are still ready to sign a fresh agreement at Rs. 12 per Kg another export-import firm, SV Exports, India, joined hands with the Government in its Government Onion Hunt on October 21.

This firm, referred to as the "private party" until today and represented by V. Sareen in Delhi, entered, into an agreement with DSCSC on October 21: they would airlift 750 tonne

* Joy Purkayastha, New Delhi, October 26.

of onion from Iran and DSCSC would buy the stock in Delhi at 700 dollar per tonne (Rs. 30 per Kg).

And the Great Onion Hunt — notwithstanding that it will now cost more than what MSM Trading had agreed on — does not stop here. DSCSC has also struck a deal with Tradeline LNC International of Dubai to import 1,000 tonne of onion by ship at 265 Dollars per tonne. This consignment is expected to reach Delhi by November 5-6.

Government Chooses Dearer Way to Get Onions*

The Delhi Government's decision to airlift onion from Iran too will cost the exchequer dear as Dubai-based company, with which it has cancelled its contract, had offered the commodity at a much lower price.

The difference in subsidy done is likely to cost an additional Rs. 5 crore as the State Government has promised to sell onions at Rs. 10 per Kg.

The Government has signed an agreement under which onions were to be delivered at Mumbai from Dubai at Rs. 10.71 per Kg. It is, however, now buying onions from Iran at Rs. 30 per Kg. As per the earlier contract, onion prices would have come to Rs. 13 per Kg while the difference in subsidy now is Rs. 17 per Kg.

Though Chief Secretary Omesh Saigal said the Government was planning to initiate penal action against the Dubai firm for "backtracking," correspondence between parties suggests otherwise.

Sources said the Delhi State Civil Supplies Corporation (DSCSC) had entered into an agreement with Dubai-based Mohd Sayeed Mattar (MSM) Trading Est for importing 3,000 tonnes of onions. The Government had decided to sell them at Rs. 10 per Kg and subsidise the remaining amount.

While the company had initially quoted $275 per tonne, the price was settled at $255 per tonne (approximately Rs. 10.71 per Kg). Transportation costs from Mumbai to Delhi would have come to Rs. 1.50 per Kg. The bulbs would have

* Rahul Pandey, New Delhi.

been available in the Capital for around Rs. 13 per Kg, involving a subsidy of Rs. 3 per Kg.

According to the terms of the agreement on October 9, a Letter of Credit (LoC) was to be opened on October 10. The Dubai company was to be given three days to set the shipment sailing and the onions were to arrive in Delhi by October 19. The DSCSC opened the LoC two days late (in the evening of October 12) and in the wrong name. While the firm was called MSM Trading Est, the LoC was opened in the name of MSM Est, making the document invalid. This mistake notwithstanding, the company was asked to ensure that onion-laden ships left Dubai port by 5 pm on October 13.

With the LoC being corrected later, the shipment deadline was extended to October 16. The LoC expiry date was also extended to October 20. The company, however, alleged that there was no time to confirm the LoC, which could take up to five days to clear.

Company officials, corresponding with the DSCSC, indicated that since bank norms in Dubai were different from those in New Delhi, a "strong" LoC was necessary.

With subsequent paperwork failing to change the situation, the company officials indicated that problems had arisen because of DSCSC's ignorance of international trade norms.

On October 18, meanwhile, the Delhi Government decided to airlift onions from Iran. It was indicated that 750 tonnes would be airlifted at Rs. 30 per Kg. Problems with the original LoC have created a situation whereby DSCSC would end up buying 750 tonnes of onions, worth Rs. 2.25 crore, while it could have managed 3,000 tonnes for nearly Rs. 3.25 crore. Besides, the corporation would have to pay over Rs. 1.25 crore as additional subsidy on the purchase of 750 tonnes.

Crisis Management of Onions*

The present government, instead of resorting to desperate measures to contain the onion prices should take a lesson from one particular Sultan who successfully introduced certain market regulations, suggests Vijaya Ramaswamy.

---

* *The Hindustan Times*, New Delhi, Sunday October 18, 1998.

Onions may hold the key to the present political situation. The forthcoming assembly elections in Delhi, Rajasthan and Madhya Pradesh may be decisively influenced by the shortage of onions and its sky high price (Rs. 45 per Kg). If onion prices are touching the sky the other vegetables are not far behind. Cauliflower at Rs. 40, potatoes and lady's fingers at Rs. 20 are no less daunting. In a spiralling effect the prices of wheat and oil have also shot up with wheat flour selling at Rs. 30 a Kg in contrast to Rs. 20 last year while refined oil sells at Rs. 55 which sold at Rs. 40 last year. The soaring prices in Delhi reminds one of an old English nursery rhyme

"Hey diddle diddle, the cat and the fiddle,The cow jumped over the moon"

The reference was to the soaring beef prices in England. Needless to say, as prices rose governments fell. The time has indeed come for the BJP Government to take lessons from history.

Delhi in the time of the Khiljis was going through a terrible inflation. The price rise was primarily caused by the political exigencies of the 14th century. The Mongol threat on the borders of the Sultanate could only be tackled by having an army in readiness at Delhi. The presence of a huge band of a salaried soldiers mulling around in the streets of Delhi begun to push prices up. An inflationary situation in the market logically led to the similar situations of artificial scarcity, hoarding and black-marketing. The soldiers as well as the masses became discontented as their purchasing power dropped. The rising tide of anger against the government could not have been very different from what it is today.

In this zigzag exercise through time one encounters the problem of price imbalances in both situations, the present as well as the medieval past. The situation of acute scarcity in Delhi and Maharashtra is set off by the glut in other places leading to a sharp fall in prices and the destruction of crops in what has been called a reverse Malthusian phenomenon. To quote a recent headline, "As Delhi Suffers, Shimla Enjoys an Onion Feast". (The Times of India, Delhi Times, 30 September). It is indeed amazing that while the price of onions in Delhi average between Rs. 45 to 50 per Kg, in the neighbouring area of Shimla, barely 200 km away, the same vegetable sells at Rs. 12 per Kg. Delhi in the time of Ala ud din Khilji went through a similar crisis with grain and vegetables selling at one third the price in the countryside while people buy onions even at Rs. 70 per Kg in Delhi. In striking contrast the medieval Sultan managed to hold the price line and successfully checked the rising tide of discontent. The Sultanate historian Zia ud din Barani provides the most colourful description of the market regulations of Ala ud din Khilji.

First the Sultanate administration issued a rate list for various commodities recording the optimum sale price of essential items including grain, oil and cloth. From the entire countryside (the Ganga-Jamuna doab being a principal supplier) farmers were only allowed to sell their products at official outlets at governmental rates. In order to control and regulate food supply and prices, Banjara merchants transporting grain over long distance (Multani merchants in case of cloth) were officially registered. A special officer called Shahna was appointed to see that there was no attempt to hoard or indulge in black-marketing. Spies disguised as potential customers were sent to keep a watch on the retailers. Hoarders and profiteers met with summary punishment. Rationing was introduced in addition to private control to ensure that consumers did not indulge in panic hoarding. Barani says that as a consequence of these swift and efficient measures the prices stabilised with wheat selling at just 7 jitals per man (a moaned being roughly 88 seers to the Rupee in terms of 14th century values) while barley sold at 4 jitals per man and good quality rice for just 5 jitals per man.

Onion Crisis: Minister Wrings her Hands in Despair*

Despite desperate attempts by the Delhi Government to reduce soaring prices of onions, potatoes, tomatoes, pulses and edible oil, the situation seems to have gone out of control. With the Delhiites agitated over the steep prices, there is a panic reaction in the Bharatiya Janata Party that the uncon-

* By Anju Sharma, New Delhi, October 29.

trolled prices may affect their prospects in the forthcoming Assembly elections.

The prices of onions in the retail market continue to hover at Rs. 50–60 per Kg in most areas of the Capital. Sushma Swaraj's claim that onion prices would be brought down has proved wrong. The much-touted import of onions from Iran has also failed to yield results.

While imported onions from Iran are yet to reach the Delhi market, 75 tonnes of onions from Tajakistan were released in the market today. However, even the wholesale prices of onions at the Azadpur mandi for a 40 Kg sack were as steep at Rs. 650 to Rs. 1,700.

With limited supplies coming from abroad, the Delhi markets are literally onion-starved. Delhi Food and Civil Supplies Minister Poornima Sethi charged that the Congress-dominated cooperatives in the onion-rich belts of Nasik, Sangli, Dhulia and Jalgoan were preventing the supply of onions to Delhi. "It is plain politics. Since these Congress-dominated cooperatives have purchased a large number of onion fields they are not allowing the supply of onions to Delhi for political reasons," she added.

The Delhi Government officials had dashed to Bangalore to purchase onions. However, the trip has proved to be a futile one. "Again vested interests in the Karnataka Government are not allowing onion supplies to begin from Bangalore," Ms. Sethi said, adding that in the domestic markets, Delhi was receiving supply only from Khairthwal near Alwar.

Today 635 tonnes of onions reached Delhi from Alwar as against yesterday's 535 tonnes. "Since the domestic supply is limited, we are being forced to rely on imports of onions," the Minister added.

Despite onions being placed under the open general licence, hardly any private parties are importing onions into the country. Ms. Sethi claimed that limited onions were available in the foreign markets as well so it was difficult for the private businessmen to import onions.

People who buy onions from Mother Dairy, Super Bazar and the Delhi Government outlets complain that the onions are of poor quality. "The onions may be subsidised here but the quality is extremely poor. It is better to buy from the open market where the quality is slightly better," said a customer standing in a queue at the Mother Dairy outlet.

However, the Food and Civil Supplies Minister today lambasted the NAFED officials for not supporting them at this crucial stage. "Since NAFED is dominated by politically-motivated elements, they have not been supplying onions regularly to us. While NAFED should supply 150 metric tonnes onions everyday, we received only 40 metric tonnes yesterday and 60 metric tonnes today," Ms Sethi added.

Apart from onions, the high prices of potatoes, tomatoes and other vegetables are also burning holes in the pockets of Delhiites. The ban on the export of potatoes notwithstanding, the prices are soaring and the staple food is now selling at Rs. 25–30 per Kg. Last week, potatoes had been available in the markets at Rs. 6–7 per Kg. The case of tomatoes is also similar with the prices shooting to Rs. 35 per Kg. Only last week the tomatoes were selling at Rs. 16–20 per Kg.

Ms. Sethi said that if potato prices continued to rise, the Government could consider importing them to ease the situation.

Moreover, despite a ban on the export of pulses, the prices of the commodity too are soaring. The Minister admitted that the prices of *arhar dal* had risen during the last few weeks. "However, this has happened because unseasonal rains have destroyed pods of the plants thereby reducing supplies," the Minister added.

Onions to be Airlifted from Iran: Sushma*

For all the hope that the Delhi Government had held out of an improvement in the supply of onions and consequent fall in its prices, the Chief Minister, Ms. Sushma Swaraj, today conceded that the onion crisis cannot be wished away easily.

Now that supplies from Nasik have dried up — following incessant rain there — and the promise of onions from Dubai has not materialised, the Delhi Government has decided to airlift onions from Iran. But even this will take time and the

* *Hindu*, New Delhi, October 18.

earliest supply from Iran is not likely to reach the Capital before mid-week.

Announcing this at a press conference here today, the Chief Minister, Ms. Sushma Swaraj, said the Delhi Government had placed an order with Iran yesterday. Since shipping the onions to India would take time, the Government has decided to airlift four tonnes of onions daily as an interim measure till the shipment arrives.

Giving details about her Government's efforts to ease the situation at the earliest, Ms. Swaraj said, "seeing that Nasik and Dubai had failed to deliver, I spoke to the Indian Ambassador in Iran yesterday and asked him to find out whether onions were available there, its price, and the time needed for delivery". Apparently, onions are not as dear in Iran as they are in Delhi these days. A kilogram of onion in Iran today costs the equivalent of Rs. 10. The only hitch is that shipping onions to India will take a couple of weeks. Consequently, the decision to airlift the onions. Now that the Delhi Government has found another source of onions, it has decided to meet the city's total demand for four tonnes of onions daily from Iran.

Just two days ago, on Friday, Ms. Swaraj had claimed that the Central Government's decision to place onion import under Open General Licence (OGL) had borne fruit. After visiting the Agricultural Produce Marketing Committee in Azadpur Mandi on Friday, she informed the Press that in place of the earlier four trucks of onions from Nasik, on that day Delhi had received 20 vehicles of onions. She had attributed this five-fold increase in supply to the placing of onion import under OGL.

However, due to rains in Nasik, this supply line of onions to Delhi could not be taped for a day longer. Also, for reasons she did not divulge, Dubai has not delivered the onions that had been ordered from there by the National Agricultural Marketing Cooperative Federation (NAFED).

Probe Sought into Onion Purchase*

The Delhi Assembly today passed a resolution that the new government should order an enquiry into the irregularities in purchase of onions worth crores by the previous BJP Government during the tenure of Chief Minister Sushma Swaraj.

The resolution was moved by Congress member Mukesh Sharma amidst noisy scenes of protest from the Opposition during the motion of thanks to the Lt. Governor's address today.

The MLA from Hastsal alleged that during the peak crisis period of skyrocketing onion prices in Delhi last month, Chief Minister Swaraj and her associates had imported onions through the Delhi State Civil Supply Corporation in a shady deal that had caused the exchequer a loss of Rs. 13 crore.

Sharma said that her predecessor Sahib Singh had entered into an agreement with a Dubai-based party to import onions at the rate of Rs. 10.71 per Kg. However, on assuming charge as Chief Minister, Ms. Swaraj scrapped the deal and entered into an agreement with a private party to buy onions at the rate of Rs. 30 per kg instead.

Besides, he also charged that she rejected premier agency NAFED's offer to supply 2,000 metric tons of onion at Rs. 8 per Kg and preferred to buy the vegetable from her associates at Rs. 24.25 per Kg thus causing a huge loss to Delhi Government.

He demanded that the onion import scandal should be thoroughly probed and criminal cases should be registered against those found guilty. However, BJP members led by their legislature party leader Jagdish Mukhi vehemently protested against the charge calling it baseless. Mr. Mukhi challenged the Congress members to lodge a complaint with the Lokayukta of Delhi for an enquiry.

The resolution was passed after Speaker Prem Singh called for voting on it and all Congress members voted in its favour. Earlier, the Opposition had stalled the proceedings of the House for nearly 45 minutes demanding a CBI probe into the

* *The Hindustan Times*, New Delhi, December 17.

alleged recovery of hoarded pulses worth Rs. 250 crore from the mills of Congress MLA Mangat Ram Singhal.

Initiating the motion of thanks to the Lt. Governor's address, Mukesh Sharma stated that all promises made by the BJP Government during the last five years had turned out to be false and the people had voted them out of power for that reason.

The Congress Government was now committed to protecting the interests of the public and strict action would be taken against all hoarders and blackmarketeers, he said.

Rajouri Garden MLA Ajay Maken criticised the previous government for having failed to utilise the funds earmarked for various welfare schemes and reeled off concrete figures to support his argument.

In his speech, BJP legislature party leader Mukhi pointed out that in the Lt. Governor's address, which was a statement of the government's policies and programmes there was strangely not a single new plan or proposal framed by the new government. All the plans contained in the address were those that had been formed and put into motion by the BJP government during their tenure.

The BJP members later staged a walkout as the Speaker refused to allow them more time to speak in the House.

APPEAL TO THE VOTERS

PEOPLE'S COUNCIL
and the
Assembly Elections

In view of the appointment of Shrimati Sushma Swaraj, as Chief Minister of Delhi, being arbitrary, illegal, unconstitutional and against the model code of conduct, the People's Council in its emergent meeting held on 26.10.98, passed the following resolution, unanimously.

"Resolved that the Chairman of the Council, Dr. Janak Raj Jai should approach the People's Court by contesting Assembly Elections, against Smt. Sushma Swaraj, from wherever, she contests. Further resolved that the Council may put up some more candidates against the undesirable candidates, particularly those with shady antecedents, and those who are not defecto residents of Delhi."

I Janak Raj Jai, bow before the directions of the People's Council, and hereby decide to contest as People's candidate, against Smt. Sushma Swaraj, from wherever she contests in the coming Assembly Elections."

I earnestly appeal to all the political parties to extend their whole hearted support and expose BJP which is bent upon destroying the democratic norms in the National Capital Territory of Delhi. I am sure the Congress Party as also other political parties would be gracious enough to spare the seat, from which Smt. Sushma will be contesting, for me so that there is one to one, a decisive fight. Voters of Delhi, who are very wise and mature, would definitely throw her out through the Ballot, which will be an eye-opener for all times to come.

30th October, 1998 Janak Raj Jai
Chairman, People's Council

Note: Since the Congress Party in the meantime had nominated Prof. Kiran Walia, to contest from Hauz Khas against Smt. Sushma Swaraj, the People's Council decided to support Mrs. Walia wholeheartedly.

PEOPLE'S COUNCIL
C-50 Rajpur Khurd Colony
New Delhi 68
Tele 6932057, 6803447

BJP'S ACHIEVEMENTS

1. Rapes, murders, daylight robberies, kidnappings, extortion.
2. Adulterated mustard oil and dropsy death of innocent people of Delhi.
3. Deepaks without oil on Deepawali.
4. Sky-rocketing prices:-

Onion	Rs. 50–70 per Kg
Potato	Rs. 30–40 per Kg
Tomato	Rs. 30–40 per Kg
Pulses	Rs. 40–45 per Kg

5. Darkness in Delhi without Electricity.
6. Contaminated water, heaps of garbage, air pollution and noise pollution.
7. Converted Delhi into the largest slum of India.
8. Utter chaos on the roads—killing, maiming of innocent—men, women and school children by the offending vehicles, the road killers.
9. Infighting in rank and file, and change of three Chief Ministers.
10. Made Delhi a heaven for mafia and the underworld.

RESULT

Deeva gul, Bijli gul, Pani gul, Khana gul, Jeena gul and everything GUL-GUL-GUL.

APPEAL: Pull down this Government with the might of your vote on 25.11.1998.

Dr. Janak Raj Jai,
Chairman

Avtar Singh Sohal, K.G. Sharma,
Inayat Ullah, Dr. K.P. Singh,
Anwar Masood, Rajiv Jai, Puran Mehra,
Roshan Rana, Vinay Jha

APPEAL TO THE VOTERS

People's Council

Dr. Janak Raj Jai
Chairman

Vote is a trust with every citizen, and it has to be utilised in an appropriate manner, taking into consideration the best interest of the country. With the mushroom growth of the political parties, and the role of mafia, the task has become gigantic one, and it has to be accomplished without fear or favour.

Munro, a great philosopher, had rightly observed that the people never vote for a person, they vote against a person; they vote their resentment. The living example before us is the rout of the Congress during the elections after the emergency. The people then voted against the Congress and showed their resentment through ballot.

Assembly Elections in Delhi

The Legislative Assembly Elections have been declared for 25th November, 1998 in four States including National Capital Territory of Delhi. The BJP has been ruling the State since 1993. The voters brought the BJP in power in comfortable majority. The utter non-performance of the BJP during this period is before the voters, which has completely belied their hopes and expectations.

Rape, Murder, Kidnapping

Rape, murder, dacoity, kidnapping have become the order of the day. The recent murder of a candidate has put a question mark on the credibility of the ruling party. Prices of eatable articles have gone far beyond the reach of each and every citizen. And whatever one gets is fully adulterated. Dropsy deaths in the capital are a living example.

Three Chief Ministers

During this tenure, three Chief Ministers changed hands—Madan Lal Khurana, Sahib Singh Verma, and the latest Smt. Sushma Swaraj, who is not only an outsider, but a stranger in the House. She has been illegally and unconstitutionally appointed just six weeks before the elections, in gross violation of the Code of Conduct.

Sushma's Fraud

After getting herself elected as a Member of Parliament from South Delhi, she has filed her nomination paper as a member of Legislative Assembly from Hauz Khas (South Delhi). By doing so, she has played a fraud with the people, and the Constitution. She has not even resigned from the Membership of Parliament; in case she gets defeated, she goes back as a Member of Parliament. What a fraud?

Appeal to the Voters

Dear voters, the real power is in your hands, and your right decision at a right time will decide the destiny of the Capital. If you lose this opportunity, you will have to wait for another five years. The present government has miserably failed on all fronts and needs to be pulled down, through the power of your ballot, and not the bullot. The present act of yours will be an eye-opener for the next government.

Dr. Janak Raj Jai
Chairman
People's Council
Sewa Sadan, C-50, Rajpur Khurd Colony, New Delhi 110 068,
Ph.: 6932057, 6803447.

Avtar Singh Sohal	Rajiv Jai	K.G. Sharma
Inayat Ullah	Roshan Rana	Puran Mehra
	Dr. K.P. Singh	

JUDGES OF THE PEOPLE'S COURT REJECT SUSHMA'S LEADERSHIP

A Civil Writ Petition under Article 226/227 of the Constitution of India was filed by way of Public Interest Litigation in the High Court of Delhi, challenging the appointment of Shrimati Sushma Swaraj (a sitting Member of Parliament from South Delhi) as Chief Minister of Delhi replacing Chief Minister, Sahib Singh Verma, the duly elected leader of the House by the majority of the members of the Legislative Assembly. The appointment of Shrimati Sushma Swaraj was termed as illegal, arbitrary, unconstitutional and in gross violation of Article 14, 60, 164 and 239 AA of the Constitution of India, Model Code of conduct issued by the Election Commission of India and Section 43(2) of the Government of National Capital Territory of Delhi Act, 1991.

The said writ petition raised vital points of law of grave public importance for the correct interpretation of the Hon'ble High Court of Delhi. The Law points raised in the High Court were:

(1) Whether a non-member or a sitting Member of Parliament as also a sitting Union Minister of the centre can replace the sitting Chief Minister (duly elected as the Leader of the Party by a majority of MLAs, and duly appointed by the President of India) as per Article 239 AA (5) of the Constitution of India?

(2) Whether the appointment of Shrimati Sushma Swaraj, as the Chief Minister on 12th October, 1998, was not in gross violation of Section 43(2) of the Government of National Capital Territory of Delhi Act, 1991 and Art. 164(4) of the Constitution of India, particularly when the life of the

then Assembly had practically come to an end, and in any case was much less than six months?

(3) Whether Shri Sahib Singh Verma could be forced to resign without bringing a no confidence motion against him, or without the consent of the majority of the MLAs who had duly elected him their leader on the floor of the House?

(4) Whether the appointment of Shrimati Swaraj as Chief Minister was not in gross violation of the letter and spirit of all the provisions of law, Constituent Assembly Debates, principles of natural justice, equity and model code of conduct of the Election Commission of India, and was liable to be set aside by the Hon'ble High Court of Delhi?

(5) Whether Shrimati Sushma Swaraj could be legally appointed as Chief Minister at that late stage, when the term of the Assembly had practically come to an end, and the process of Election had already started after the pronouncement of fresh Elections by the Election Commission of India, for 25th November, 1998?

(6) Whether the appointment of Shrimati Sushma Swaraj, as the Chief Minister, did not amount to an act of corrupt practices, and whether it had not been made to exert influence on the voters to have better prospects in the coming elections?

(7) Whether Shrimati Sushma Swaraj had not committed the breach of trust with the electorate of South Delhi Lok Sabha Constituency, whom she had deserted half way, and violated the oath of office, which she took at the time of becoming a Member of Parliament?

(8) Whether there was not a blatant misuse of Section 43(2) of the Government of National Capital Territory Act, 1991, as also Article 164(4) of the Constitution of India?

It was also alleged in the writ petition that since the Government was aware of its poor performance on all fronts, the BJP Central Leadership got panicky, and had thus decided to change the leadership in Delhi, even after the pronouncement of the elections to be held on 25th November, 1998.

Besides Shrimati Sushma Swaraj, Shri Sahib Singh Verma, Shri Rajendra Gupta, Lt. Governor of Delhi, Union of India through Secretary, Ministry of Home Affairs, and Chief Election Commissioner of India, were also made the parties in the writ petition.

The said Writ Petition came up for hearing on 23rd October, 1998, before their Lordships, Justices, Y.K. Sabharwal and K.S. Gupta. After hearing the petitioner not even half way, the Hon'ble Court was not inclined to issue notice to the parties, and dismissed the said petition without passing a speaking order.

Happily, millions of Judges of the People's Court, had rejected the leadership of Shrimati Sushma Swaraj, during the Assembly Elections in Delhi held on 25th November, 1998. There was a complete rout of her party in the elections held under her leadership. The petitioner got a consolation that the vital points raised by him in the writ petition have been vindicated by the People's Court. The petition was filed by your own humble author.

To avoid such type of arbitrary, unconstitutional, unethical and unconventional appointments of a high office like the Chief Minister for political gains, a national debate and a suitable and specific legislation is the need of the hour.

Here are the observations of the Hon'ble High Court, on the said writ petition as published in some national newspapers:

HC Dismisses Petition against Sushma*

The Delhi High Court today dismissed a public interest litigation challenging the recent appointment of Mrs. Sushma Swaraj as Delhi's Chief Minister, after the "unceremonious removal" of her predecessor, Mr. Sahib Singh.

The litigation, filed by petitioner-in-person, Dr. Janak Raj Jai, alleged that Mrs. Swaraj's appointment, six weeks before the Assembly elections in Delhi, was "mala fide, illegal, arbitrary and unconstitutional" and was also against the Election Commission's model code of conduct.

---

* *Statesman News Service*, New Delhi, October 23.

It sought the court's directions to restrain the new chief minister from taking any policy decision or other steps which may influence the voters in her favour in the coming elections. Directions to Mrs. Swaraj to tender her resignation from the Lok Sabha before contesting the assembly elections in the Capital was also asked for in the petition.

A Division Bench comprising Mr. Justice Y.K. Sabharwal and Mr. Justice K.S. Gupta, while dismissing the litigation, held that it was based on "surmises, conjections and assumptions".

The questions raised in the petition, the Bench observed, were not constitutional but political in nature, which cannot be entertained by the court.

Dr. Jai had petitioned that in the wake of Delhi's deteriorating law and order situation, failure to check the prices of essential commodities and a number of deaths due to adulterated mustard oil, the Centre "became very upset, keeping in view the coming Assembly elections" and replaced the chief minister. "Because of poor performance on all fronts, the BJP central leadership got panicky and decided to change the leadership, after the process of election had already started," the petition said.

Subsequently it led to resentment all across the country, with an ally, the Haryana Lok Dal President, Mr. Om Prakash Chautala, threatening to withdraw support from the Centre.

Majority of the MLAs were upset over the decision and the Maha Panchayat of about 400 villages condemned the removal of Mr. Singh.

Plea against Sushma Quashed*

The Delhi High Court on Friday dismissed a petition challenging the appointment of Ms. Sushma Swaraj as Chief Minister and ruled that contentions challenging her appointment were based on "surmise, presumption and conjecture".

The Division Bench comprising acting Chief Justice Y.K. Sabharwal and Justice K.S. Gupta said the petition had "no constitutional merit but involved only political issues".

---

* *Pioneer*, 24th October, 1998.

"No political issues should be raised in the court," the Bench cautioned petitioner Janak Raj Jai while dismissing the petition.

The Petitioner termed Ms Swaraj's appointment six weeks prior to Assembly elections as "malafide, illegal, arbitrary, unconstitutional and against the model code of conduct" and sought the court's direction for her removal from office.

HC Dismisses Petition against Sushma Swaraj*

A Petition challenging the appointment of Sushma Swaraj as Delhi Chief Minister was today dismissed by the High Court saying it was based on "surmises, presumptions and conjucture".

Acting Chief Justice Y.K. Sabharwal and Justice K.S. Gupta, in their order said the petition had "no constitutional merit but involved only political issues".

"No political issues should be raised in the forum of the court the bench cautioned. The petition terming the appointment of Swaraj just six weeks before the Assembly election as "malafide, illegal, arbitrary, unconstitutional and against the model code of conduct", was filed by advocate Janak Raj Jai.

Referring to the dismissal of a similar petition by the Supreme court, at the time of replacing Deve Gowda by I.K. Gujral as P.M. the bench said "if the apex court cannot intervene in such matters, how can we interfere?"

H.C. Rejects Petition against Sushma**

The Delhi High Court today dismissed a public interest petition challenging the appointment of Ms. Sushma Swaraj as the Chief Minister of Delhi, observing that it was 'without merit'.

A Division Bench of the Court comprising Mr. Justice Y.K. Sabharwal and Mr. Justice K.S. Gupta, which dismissed the petition in limini, said the plea was based on 'surmises, assumptions and conjectures' of the petitioner.

---

* Press Trust of India, New Delhi, October 23.

** By Our Staff Reporter, *Hindu*, October 24, 1998

The issue raised in the petition was 'political and not Constitutional', the Judges observed while dismissing the petition by Dr. Janak Raj Jai, a practising lawyer.

The petitioner had urged the Court to 'declare the appointment of Ms. Swaraj as Chief Minister, six weeks before the fresh election as mala fide, illegal, arbitrary, unconstitutional and against the model code of conduct'.

The petitioner had further prayed to the Court to restrain Ms. Swaraj from taking any policy decision, or take any step which may influence the voters in favour of her party, in the coming Assembly elections and direct her to tender resignation from the Lok Sabha before contesting in the coming elections, and hold the removal of Mr. Sahib Singh Verma illegal and unconstitutional.

After the debacle of the BJP in the Assembly Elections, Mrs. Sushma Swaraj, as earlier predicted by the author, has resigned from the membership of Legislative Assembly, and retained her seat as a Member of Parliament. The voters of Hauz Khas Constituency have once again been to he held on 22nd February, 1999. A specific legislation is the need of the hours, to avoid such type of unwarranted and unethical acts and played by unscrupulous politicians.

MEDIA REPORTS

Winner Takes it All*

After a windall victory in the Assembly elections he is set to play a major role if the Congress comes to power at the Centre. Though blessed with the height of a basketball player (6 ft 2 in), Madhya Pradesh Chief Minister Digvijay Singh had for long been vertically disadvantaged—in political terms—by too many "tall Congressmen" from his state. Arjun Singh, Shyama Charan Shukla, Vidya Charan Shukla, Motilal Vora—they're legion. However, in the assembly polls in November Digvijay, or Diggy Raja, netted the clinching point as he snatched the state from the jaws of the BJP which was banking upon an anti-incumbency wave. The victory put the scion of the princely family of Raghogarh in Congress President Sonia Gandhi's A-team. She patted him on the back in the gaze of television cameras, and his selection for the second term was hitchless, though not without the envious frowns. An astute state-level politician, Digvijay has seen Madhya Pradesh's towering Congressmen losing their popular base, and bargaining power, after being sucked into national politics. The 52-year-old politician now wants to preserve his state citadel even though the party, which stands a good chance of capturing power at the Centre, may require his talent in Delhi. Keen not to lose his grip on home turf, Digvijay says, "In the next five years, I must take Madhya Pradesh out of the BIMARU trap and convert it into a model state."

---

* Digvijay Singh

The Year that was-1998?*

The Countdown for 1998 has begun with only a few days remaining before we usher in the last year of this century. The millennium fever has gripped a large number of people as we prepare ourselves to enter the year 2000. There is so much to look back in this century and so much to look forward to in the next.

Time really flies and as Omar Khayyam said, "the moving finger writes on and having written moves on, nor all thy piety shall lure it back to cancel half a line nor all thy tears wash out a word of it". This is life and movement forward is the essence of it.

Coming back to 1998, Delhiites witnessed the change of government at the venture first followed by a change of government in the city. The Onion became the symbol of the failure of the BJP government in Delhi which faltered on many fronts before bowing out in November end.

The power and water crisis, the deteriorating law and order and crime situation, the agitation by teachers, nurses and doctors and the poor condition of educational institutions, hospitals and administrative machinery all contributed to the downfall of the BJP in the city which had voted for the Saffron brigade only eight months before to give them six out of seven seats in Parliament. The return of the Congress in the city was as much due to the strings of failure of the BJP government as it was to the new leadership provided by Ms. Sonia Gandhi who played the most important role in the comeback staged by her party in the capital after a gap of nearly nine years. She also hand picked Ms. Sheila Dikshit, the DPCC Chief to head the Congress government in Delhi thereby preferring her to all established leaders of the party in the city. The Congress under her had to have a new look and Ms. Dikshit is the face she has projected.

On the BJP front, there were several developments which showed the party in poor light. The party with a difference became a party with differences as intense factional fights hogged down the chances of its candidates in the polls. The

* *The Hindustan Times*, dated 27.12.98.

myth about the Sangh Parivar being a disciplined lot exploded and BJP leaders attacked each other openly. The gamble of installing Ms. Sushma Swaraj as the first woman Chief Minister of Delhi boomeranged badly and the Central leadership had to eat a humble pie. In the process Ms. Swaraj's political career which was on the upswing received a setback for the first time in many years and from all available indications, her innings as a representative of the people of Delhi may have ended.

The decision by Ms. Swaraj to resign her seat from the Delhi Assembly after winning from Hauz Khas by a slender margin was a classic example of a politician's belief in the credo, "have your cake and eat it too". She also put off many of her admirers by swearing on the Gita which was uncalled for. She may have to remain on the sidelines for some time now.

Mr. Madan Lal Khurana and Mr. Sahib Singh Verma succeeded in cancelling each other out. While Mr. Verma prevented Mr. Khurana from returning to the Chief Minister's chair in Delhi, Mr. Khurana blocked his entry into the Cabinet. In addition, Mr. Verma did not contest the Assembly polls and thus is no longer a member of the House. Mr. Khurana on the other hand survived politically and continues to be in the Union Cabinet though he too did not acquit himself with any credit during the winter session of Parliament. His ministry also bungled on business transactions and the government had its embarrassing moments especially on the issue of Deputy Speaker and the Patents Bill. On the administrative front, Delhi got a new Lt. Governor in Mr. Vijai Kapoor after the BJP government came to power at the Centre. A highly rated bureaucrat, Mr. Kapoor's appointment was welcomed in all quarters. But he too was unable to prevent the slide of the Delhi government on various fronts. The things had gone so bad that the entire work culture in the city's administration was missing. The city also got a new Police Commissioner as Mr. T.R. Kakkar was replaced by his number two, Mr. V.N. Singh. However, the crime situation did not show any signs of improvement as murders and robberies showed a marked increase. The respect for the Khaki uniform also diminished and the prime example of this was when an ACP on probation was mauled by a bad character in West Delhi.

The Home Ministry's policy over police postings drew a lot of criticism and some officers who could have been assets to the city were transferred out soon after their return to the cadre while some others who have never done any hard postings were permitted to stay on despite the fact that they have nothing much to show.

The dropsy epidemic made the entire country hang its head in shame as the authorities were unable to check the sale of contaminated mustard oil which sent many victims to hospital. The collapse of the public distribution system as well as the inability of those at the helm of affairs to check the prices also contributed to the woes of the people. The onion thus became a symbol of the failures.

On the Congress front, Ms. Dikshit's rise in local politics symbolised the downfall of all established Congress leaders for the time being. Stalwarts like Mr. H.K.L. Bhagat, Mr. Sajjan Kumar, Mr. Jagdish Tytler and Mr. J.P. Aggarwal may find it extremely hard to make comeback on the city scene as they do not seem to be fitting the scheme of things of Ms. Sonia Gandhi.

As far as Ms. Dikshit is concerned, she may have the patronage of the high command but she may not find the going very easy in the city about whose politics she does not know much even though she had been catapulted to the centrestage. She has to move very carefully in order to retain the popularity her party got during these elections and has to side step sycophants, power brokers and favour seekers. Delhi has been the city of power brokers for centuries and the cult of sycophancy is a part of its history and culture.

Whether it is the BJP which may be in power or the Congress, the power brokers always have played an important role. How else could someone like Romesh Sharma who also hit headlines this year become so important and powerful. Romesh Sharma is also a symbol of the power culture of this city. There are several Romesh Sharmas who are moving about unchecked and are achieving what they wish to achieve.

In the eighties, a well attended party at a Mehrauli farm house had attracted media attention when a large number of bureaucrats, politicians and influential people gathered at the farm house of a person once described in political and social circles as the Cadilac pimp. Around the same time, a sensational espionage case featuring the personal staff of the principal secretary to the Prime Minister had also hit the headlines. Popularly known as the Coomar Narain scandal, the case showed how an operating through wine, women and wealth had totally established a stranglehold over the PMO. Such unmarked Coomar Narains or Romesh Sharmas continue to operate in the city.

The latest in bureaucratic circles is a certain Baba who operates from near Mehrauli. According to available information, many top bureaucrats and police officials visit him regularly and he guides them in shaping their destiny.

The novel technique he adopts is that he makes his visitors first smell his shoe before he reels off what is in store for them in the power circles.

Bureaucrats and Police officials of the Union Territory cadre have also been depended on long for transfers, postings and other favours on a well turned out man who owns a shop in Chandni Chowk. With his bubbly style, he has access to the houses of most officials and does all kinds of odd jobs for them. At one time, most officials of the Delhi government and its allied agencies used to keep table diaries provided by him on their official desks.

Therefore, those in power must know that there could be a Romesh Sharma waiting to way lay them at every given opportunity. The CM and her colleagues must know whose invitation to accept or whose to turn down. Model Town residents for instance were surpassed when a senior functionary attended a party hosted by a man whose credentials are dubious.

The new year is about to commence. It is therefore time to make new resolutions and execute them. May 1999 be the year to remember for all Delhiites. When I say it, I mean it in the positive sense. Happy New Year. Between us.

Pankaj Vohra

Memories 1998—Flops of the Year*

So tangible was Mr. Atal Behari Vajpayee's appeal in the run-up to the 1998 Lok Sabha elections that the 'Ab Ki Barri Atal Behari' slogan found resonance in the poll outcome all over India. It was this crucial factor that enabled the saffron party to win friends among parties—with whom secularism was an article of faith—and post surpass victories in uncharted territories and states.

The Vajpayee persona was a factor, however negligible, even in the DMK-TMC's rout by the AIADMK-led front in Tamil Nadu. As Andhra Pradesh rooted for the BJP mascot, even that leading impresario of the secular versus communal debate, N. Chandrababu Naidu, couldn't dare coming in the way of Atalji's Raj Tilak. The TDP's issue-based support to him was dictated as much by public mood as by the Chief Minister's political needs.

Karnataka, Uttar Pradesh, Bihar and Orissa were among the other States where the electorate fell for the BJP's promise of a stable government under an able Premier. But stability and good government have eluded the multi-party regime since its inauguration last March.

So steep has been the Central Government's fall in public esteem that the saffron party has lost power in two States—Rajasthan and Delhi—without being able to dislodge a seemingly unpopular Congress administration in Madhya Pradesh.

The anti-incumbency factor that consumed the BJP in the Assembly polls was only compounded by the Centre's non-performance.

So insulated was Mr. Vajpayee from the ground realities that he cocked a snook at the Congress' fetish for onions, flaunting instead before a silently livid electorate his 'attainments' in the nuclear field.

The strategy was destined to boomerang. Frequent power cuts in the wake of Pokhran II had spawned countless jokes in power deficient Delhi and Rajasthan about a nuclear weapons status India.

---

* Vinod Sharma

The Vajpayee Government, it would seem, has failed on all fronts: Diplomatic, economic, political and domestic.

There has been a spurt in the attacks on minorities, farmers are buying fertiliser in the black market, prices continue to rise, indiscipline is growing in the Armed Forces and a nuclearised south Asia has only attracted sharper world focus on the festering Kashmir problem.

Even in the legislative sphere, the ruling combine is being led by the nose by the Congress, which only hopes to immunise the electorate against the BJP by prolonging the lame-duck Vajpayee Government's stay in power.

The cracks within the Sangh Parivar are widening with every passing day, the RSS distancing itself from the Centre's 'anti-swadeshi' liberalisation thrust and its sister outfits, such as the Vishwa Hindu Parishad and the Bajrang Dal, relentlessly pursuing their Hindutva line.

BJP lost in Capital's Political Wilderness*

Two new faces made their foray into Delhi politics, one of them, Mrs. Sheila Dikshit, ending up basking in the new-found glory and the other, wondering what went wrong.

The latter, Mrs. Sushma Swaraj, has company. The year also saw the political futures of many a veteran politician of the Capital turning topsy-turvy. The former Chief Minister, Mr. Sahib Singh, who was on his way to project himself as a national leader, saw his plans being nipped in the bud. The year did not go well for his predecessor in the Chief Minister's chair, Mr. Madan Lal Khurana, either. But Mr. Khurana still had the Union Minister's chair to break the fall.

A relative newcomer to the twists and turns in Delhi politics, Mrs. Sheila Dikshit took her detractors—even within the Congress—by surprise when she romped back with 51 of the 69 Assembly seats and was elected the Leader of the Congress Legislature Party.

The Congress' tally was two more than the Bharatiya Janata party's 49 seats in the 1993 Delhi Assembly elections,

* *Statesman News Service,* New Delhi, December 30.

when BJP fortune was at its peak. The "high spirit" in the BJP camp had continued till the middle of this year.

In the parliamentary elections this year, the BJP had managed to mop up six of the seven Lok Sabha seats. And then, the BJP's popularity chart took a downswing — a power and water crisis in summer, 67 deaths due to adulterated mustard oil and followed by the failure to arrest price rise of food items, specially onions.

In the meantime, things had started looking up for Congress.

Mrs. Sheila Dikshit took over as the Delhi Congress President and with the party president, Mrs. Sonia Gandhi's backing, was able to stem factionalism in the State unit.

The BJP was under pressure. Mr. Madan Lal Khurana wanted to be reinstated as Chief Minister and convinced the party leadership to replace Mr. Sahib Singh. The BJP faltered and replaced Mr. Singh on eve of elections. But with another Union Minister, Mrs. Sushma Swaraj.

Crestfallen at the turn of events, Mr. Khurana and Mr. Singh largely kept away from campaigning, except where their favourites were contesting. They did not have anything at stake.

The BJP and Mr. Singh's replacement, Mrs. Swaraj, had but found themselves unable to check the downswing in the party's popularity. Mrs. Swaraj was a leader without mass following and Delhiites were unimpressed with her stunts. This time round, even BJP workers—piqued at having been taken for granted by the leaders—were in no mood to help out the party.

The Congress won hands down. Mrs. Sheila Dikshit's entry, an impressive one at that, however, took its toll on the faces Delhi Congress had been associated for just about two decades—Mr. H.K.L. Bhagat, Mr. Jagdish Tytler and Mr. Sajjan Kumar.

The latter, however, played his cards well and projected himself as the man behind Mrs. Dikshit's success and her loyalist. Politically, Mr. Bhagat is a spent force and Mr. Tytler is expected to make a comeback bid. That, however, will be next year.

I-T official Complains to EC about CM-Romesh 'Nexus'—Gupta Wants his Transfer to be Stayed—Sushma Ready to Battle it out in Court*

Charging Chief Minister Sushma Swaraj with protecting the notorious Dawood Ibrahim aid Romesh Sharma, Additional Commissioner (Income Tax) Vishv Bandhu Gupta has petitioned Chief Election Commissioner (CEC) M.S. Gill to stay his transfer from the South Zone.

In the petition, to Mr. Gill today, Mr. Gupta has alleged that the Chief Minister has been leading a "personal campaign" against him to protect Romesh Sharma's interests.

He indicated that he was transferred from the South Zone within 24 hours of Ms. Swaraj becoming the Chief Minister because she needed money for the forthcoming Assembly elections.

Reacting sharply to Mr. Gupta's letter, Ms. Sushma Swaraj dared him to move the court and said it was very unfair that his transfer was being linked with Romesh Sharma.

"Why is he writing to the CEC? Let him move the court, I'll deal with him there. I don't understand why he is linking this episode with Romesh Sharma. I have nothing to do with Romesh Sharma. I have never met him or spoken with him. I had written a letter to former Prime Minister I.K. Gujral asking him to initiate an enquiry against Vishva Bandhu Gupta because people in my constituency had complained against him. That was more than a year back. I do not know why that letter is being reproduced and distorted in such a fashion," Ms. Swaraj said.

Meanwhile, Mr. Gupta has urged Mr. Gill to take an immediate action in this regard as the transfer order came after the announcement of elections in Delhi which, he said, is a violation of the code of conduct issued by the Election Commission.

"It is evident from Ms. Swaraj's own admission that she had been leading a personal campaign against me ever since I took over as Additional Commissioner in South Delhi only to protect the interests of several leading tax evaders, hawala

---

By Poornima Joshi, New Delhi, November 2

racketeers and criminals like Romesh Sharma. Many of these criminals including Romesh Sharma had been facing prosecution when I was abruptly transferred. Chief Commissioner Raj Narain was in such a hurry to transfer me out that he got the administrative office opened for this specific purpose. The office was closed in the afternoon that day," Mr. Gupta alleged in the petition.

Mr. Gupta also accused the Chief Minister of associating closely with most hawala dealers and criminals like Romesh Sharma because she needed money for the elections.

"The fact that the transfer orders came within 24 hours of her assuming the Chief Minister's office is no coincidence is quite evident from the fact that Ms. Swaraj needed large sums of money for the 70 Assembly constituencies in which the Bharatiya Janata Party (BJP) is going to field candidates. The dubious owner of a guest house in South Extension-II has constantly been her main conduit between tax-evaders, hawala operators and criminals, evidence in regard to which is now available with us. The relentless campaign against me could only have been propelled by a powerful concern—the concern of powerful tax-evaders, hawala racketeers and criminals," he charged.

Calling her a "habitual liar" Mr. Gupta said that Ms. Swaraj was well aware of Romesh Sharma's nefarious activities in her constituency but she swung into action only after he got his properties and helicopter attached and impounded. "Ms Sushma Swaraj is a habitual liar. She used her substantial political power to get me transferred from South Zone.

Police Report Says Romesh met Sushma*

The Delhi Police's interrogation report of Romesh Sharma sent to some investigating agencies categorically states that he had claimed to have met former Delhi Chief Minister Sushma Swaraj a few days before he was arrested by the police.

It may be recalled that Ms. Swaraj had sworn over the Bhagwad Gita in public that she did not know Romesh Sharma.

---

* Madhukar Kumar, New Delhi, January 4.

She had done so on the eve of the Delhi Assembly polls and maintained ever since that she had never heard of him.

She also added that her husband, Swaraj Kaushal, had ever met him. So now the above mentioned report could cast a shadow over her future political career.

"Romesh Sharma had told us during interrogation that he knew Sushma Swaraj and that a few days before he was arrested, he had met the former Chief Minister," said an officer who questioned Romesh. He had also stated that he had met her on a few occasions before. His claim was as vehement as the denial of Ms. Swaraj, he added.

Sources in intelligence agencies who are in possession of the report said that Romesh had also told the sleuths during interrogation that three days after he met Ms. Swaraj, Additional Commissioner Income Tax, Vishva Bandhu Gupta, was transferred out. Mr. Gupta was investigating some cases against Romesh at that time.

The interrogation report, the sources said, further names several politicians who had "close links" with Romesh. The investigating agencies had been asked to prepare a list of the people who were close to Romesh Sharma.

Police Asked to Explain Romesh-Sushma Leak*

Delhi police commissioner V.N. Singh and other senior Delhi police officials were on Tuesday summoned by senior North Block officials to explain how the name of former Delhi Chief Minister Sushma Swaraj as one of the persons invovled in the Romesh Sharma case was disclosed to the press.

According to a report which appeared in a city newspaper on Tuesday, a police interrogation report of Mr. Sharma "categorically states that he (Mr. Sharma) had met Ms. Swaraj a few days before he was arrested (on October 20)."

The report also said that Mr. Sharma has told the police officials that he had met Ms. Swaraj on several occasions.

Till the time of going to press, there was no denial of the story either by Ms. Swaraj or by the Delhi police. During the run up to the November Assembly Elections, Ms. Swaraj had

---

* *The Asian Age*, 6.1.99.

sworn on the Gita that neither she nor her husband Swaraj Kaushal have any links with Mr. Sharma.

Throughout Tuesday, there was hectic activity in the North Block offices of the ministry of home affairs. Mr. V.N. Singh and some other senior Delhi police officials were summoned in the afternoon and asked how the police interrogation report got leaked.

Under instructions, several phones have also been put under surveillance to find out how the police interrogation report was leaked.

According to sources, Union Home Minister L.K. Advani, who had publically announced he would "expose the godfathers" of Mr. Sharma in the run up to the November Assembly elections, is now finding it difficult to continue the thorough probe as he is not getting the right inputs from officials.

At almost every public platform during the campaigning for the November polls, Mr. Advani had promised to get to the bottom of the case. He had also planned to bring out a white paper on the issue as the matter relates to internal security but the paper was not placed in Parliament, even a white paper on ISI activities could not be placed in the recently concluded Winter Session. Meanwhile, the Delhi police has registered one more case of robbery and extortion against Mr. Sharma. The case has been registered on the basis of a complaint filed by a Mumbai-based architect. The case was filed on Monday at the Hauz Khas police station in South Delhi after the recent complaint by architect Dinky Mascaranhas.

In his complaint, Mr. Mascaranhas has alleged that Mr. Sharma contacted him in November 1996 through his friend Samuel Bandish for drawing architectural plans for his (Mr. Sharma's) Jai Mata Di farm-house on the outskirts of Delhi and his other properties. Mr. Bandish is a car dealer of Juhu, Mumbai.

Mr. Mascaranhas came to Delhi with the plans which had cost him Rs. 4 lakhs. It is alleged that Mr. Sharma, in the presence of two persons identified as Vinod Luthra, alias Billu, and Arvind Bali, asked him to sign an agreement to sell two floors of his property in Mumbai.

Mr. Mascaranhas owns two floors in Harshad Kunj, Mumbai. It is alleged that Mr. Sharma gave him a draft of Rs. 5 lakhs and forced him to sign advance receipts at gunpoint. The Mumbai-based architect has alleged that he was robbed of his cell phone and after the incident he started receiving threats on the phone by Chota Shakeel, a member of Dubai-based Dawood Ibrahim gang.

Mr. Mascaranhas, in his complaint, said that he did not report the matter to the police at that time as he received threatening calls from Chota Shakeel. The complainant also alleged that Mr. Sharma robbed him of two Chevrolet cars in March 1998, when he had brought them for sale here and forced him to sign a receipt for Rs. 1.28 crores. The victim mustered courage to file a complaint only after Mr. Sharma was arrested by the Delhi police.

The police said that the two Chevrolet cars were seized by the Delhi police from Mr. Sharma's Mayfair Garden residence during the raid on October 21, 1998. With this robbery and extortion case, the total number of cases against Mr. Sharma soon after his arrest on October 21, of which 13 are under investigation by the Delhi police while the other two have been transferred to the CBI. Those transferred to the CBI pertain to forcible acquisition of a helicopter belonging to H. Suresh Rao and obtaining by "questionable means" a passport for Dawood Ibrahim's mother during July 1993.

His detention under the National Security Act has been, however, revoked following rejection of his detention on "technical grounds" by an advisory board of the Delhi high court.

During the searches at Mr. Sharma's house, jointly by Delhi police, income tax, excise and wildlife officials, documents pertaining to at least 11 properties in Delhi and five in Mumbai were found.

In addition, 14 cars, imported liquor, animal skins, 14 live cartridges of .32 bore, jewellery, gold crockery and other precious ornaments, Rs. 11 lakh in cash and shares worth Rs. 1 crore and FDRs for Rs. 23.50 lakh were recovered.

Romesh's Cassettes Handed Over to Home Secretary*

Home secretary B.P. Singh has been given the police reports and cassettes of the interrogation of Mr. Romesh Sharma after the sensational leak of one of the reports in which Mr. Sharma has confessed that he met former Delhi Chief Minister Sushma Swaraj a few days before he was arrested.

The news was carried in a leading English daily earlier this week. The news report, quoting police interrogation reports of Mr. Sharma, "categorically states that he (Mr. Sharma) had met Ms. Swaraj a few days before he was arrested (on October 20)." The news report also said that Mr. Sharma has told the police officials that he had met Ms. Swaraj on several occasions.

There was no denial of the news report from either the Delhi Police or Ms. Swaraj herself.

Immediately after the report was published, Delhi Police chief V.N. Singh was summoned by senior North Block officials and asked to explain how the report got leaked.

On Wednesday, the home secretary also asked for the relevant interrogation reports and cassettes in which Mr. Sharma speaks about his links with Ms. Swaraj. The documents and cassettes were delivered to Mr. Singh on Wednesday evening.

According to sources, the Delhi Lieutenant-Governor Vijai Kapoor has also been asking for the relevant reports since Tuesday.

Home Minister L.K. Advani after handing over the probe in the Sharma case to the Inter-Departmental Group had publically announced that Ms. Swaraj has no links with Mr. Sharma. However, during the run up to Delhi Assembly elections in November, the issue of Ms. Swaraj's links with Mr. Sharma came up in a big way and neither Mr. Advani nor Ms. Swaraj's public denial helped salvage the party's image. It was only after Prime Minister Atal Behari Vajpayee, after checking with North Block officials, also gave a clean chit to Ms. Swaraj, that the issue died out.

---

* *The Asian Age*, dated 8.1.99.

According to a senior North Block officer, the home secretary has the right to ask for the interrogation reports and there is nothing "unusual" about it. However, the sources added that the home minister desires to see the report and the cassettes and that the home secretary acted under his directions. When contacted, Delhi Police officials refused to comment on it.

Disappointed Sushma Quits Assembly Seat

Two hours after Sushma Swaraj was not sworn in as a Union Cabinet minister, the ousted CM of Delhi gave up her Assembly seat. She now remains a member of the Lok Sabha from the South Delhi constituency of Hauz Khas.

At approximately the time when Pramod Mahajan was formally taking over her former portfolio as Information and Broadcasting Minister, Swaraj was spending a wintry evening in her silent home on Tees January Marg. There were no visitors, in stark contrast from before polls. "I had to resign one seat, either the Assembly or Parliament. I met Vajpayeeji at 10 a.m. today and he asked me to quit from the Assembly."

"It is not like I am unemployed or something," she says defensively. "I am still the member of the Lok Sabha and I will start attending the House from Monday."

She has left it to Vajpayee to find her the right portfolio. Asked if she may be accommodated as a minister of state, she replied: "There is no precedence of a Cabinet Minister being reinstated as a minister of state. It would not be keeping in with my status." But she quickly added: "It is Vajpayeeji's prerogative." There is a world of difference between this subdued voice and the one that a few weeks ago was forcefully promising better governance for the city. "It was a massive rout," she says reflectively, "and it was not all because of nature and price rise."

She was brought in as the CM 40 days before the Assembly elections to rescue what was termed in the BJP itself as a "government out of control" headed by Sahib Singh.

---

* Kota Neelima, New Delhi, December 5.

She smiles sadly and says, "Delhiites never gave us the chance to govern. If we had come to power, we would have given a better government." And she is a woman who has felt the anger of her voter. "When a voter in Delhi wants power, they better get it."

She also has a warning for her successor: "Sheila should not be too happy. We are going to have our summer very soon; this is just the winter."

Sahib Resigned, Cronies Fret & Fume*

The mood was defiant amongst the supporters of former Delhi Chief Minister Sahib Singh Verma who were camping outside his residence today. Inside, Mr. Verma was in a dejected and ponderous mood surrounded by his family members and close friends.

As the news of Mr. Verma's removal as Delhi's Chief Minister spread last night, thousands of supporters primarily from the Jat farmer-dominated areas of the Outer Delhi constituency and neighbouring areas in Haryana and Uttar Pradesh started pouring in.

In the morning, the supporters blocked traffic on the busy Ring Road. After an hour the police managed to convince them to move into the Sham Nath Marg area which was then closed to traffic.

At Mr. Verma's residence, where anti-central leadership and anti-Khurana posters had been put up, some supporters had managed to set up a public address system over which slogans against the central leadership were broadcast. A boisterous female supporter was entrusted with the task and through her slogans, she invoked the farmer and Jat might.

The general refrain was that Mr. Verma's supporters would not let him move out of the Chief Ministerial residence. "Our leader has been shedding tears," said one supporter from Tikri village in Outer Delhi. "How can we see this and keep quiet? Let Advani or Vajpayee come to our village, we will tell them that now we will not vote for the BJP."

---

* *The Hindustan Times* Correspondent, New Delhi, October 11.

Haryana Vikas Party (HVP) leader Om Prakash Chautala, reportedly assured Mr. Verma last night of his support. There were rumours that he would withdraw support to the Central Government in protest against Mr. Verma's removal. It was also rumoured that at least 15 Delhi MLAs turned up at Mr. Verma's residence this morning and expressed their wish to resign. However, Mr. Verma dissuaded them.

Meanwhile Mr. Verma remained cloistered with his family in some inner sanctum while the rest of his official residence swarmed with supporters and mediapersons. He periodically emerged to talk to them and generally favour his support.

Speaking to The Hindustan Times, Mr. Verma said that he had submitted his resignation to the Lt. Governor in the morning.

"They (the central leadership of the BJP) have offered me a seat in the Cabinet. No portfolio has as yet been mentioned specifically. I have not decided till now whether I will accept this offer or not", said Mr. Verma.

Regarding Ms. Sushma Swaraj, Mr. Verma said, "Yes, Ms. Swaraj's interest for the last several years, has been at the Central level only. In addition to this, she is new to Delhi, she has done her grass roots politics in Haryana only, where she was also at one time a minister in the State Government. However, since the party has chosen her over me, I am sure she will able to do the job in the coming elections. I, for one, will lend her total support as I am a loyal soldier of my party. I will do as my generals command me. However, I am basically a grass root person and will feel out of place at the central level."

Speculating on the reason for the change, Mr. Verma said, "There was a feeling in the party that the BJP would not fare well in the coming State Assembly elections under my leadership. I, personally, find no substance in it. I was confident of getting at least 55 seats. Now, if the party performs better, it might become 60. That's all."

Sahib Replaced to Avoid Defeat: Cong*

The city Congress on Tuesday termed the change of Chief Minister as a knee-jerk reaction by the Bharatiya Janata Party to avoid defeat in the November 25 hustings.

A meeting of the representatives of the 140 urbanised villages of the city were held at the party headquarters on Tuesday.

The meeting was presided over by Delhi party chief Sheila Dikshit and attended among others by former Union Minister K. Natwar Singh.

The meeting also unanimously passed a resolution demanding setting-up of an Urban Villages Development Home for the development of the urbanised village. The resolution demanded that the said Board should have a corpus of Rs. 25 crore.

Speaking on the occasion Ms. Dikshit said with the development of posh colonies the urbanised villages have been turned into slums with no civic facilities whatsoever.

Mr. Natwar Singh, in his speech, said the recent developments in the city would see an upswing in the fortunes of the Congress.

Sahib Honoured: Former Chief Minister Sahib Singh was gifted an Ambassador car and a Maruti Gypsy on Tuesday by the people of Shalimar Bagh-Pritam Pura and Outer Delhi areas for campaigning in the constituency in November 25 assembly elections.

The keys of the two cars were handed over to him at his Shalimar Bagh residence. Mr. Sahib Singh vacated the official residence on Monday after new Chief Minister Sushma Swaraj assumed office.

Sahib supporters who had gathered at his residence said the people gifted the two vehicles after he travelled by bus to his flat in Shalimar Bagh since he did not own a car.

Soon as Mr. Singh relinquished office he had surrendered his official vehicles and other privileges which were attached with the CM office.

Pioneer, New Delhi, 14.10.98.

While accepting the vehicles, Mr. Singh said he would utilise these only during electioneering and would return them as soon as the elections were over.

Sahib Says he Lacked Somewhere*

Former Delhi Chief Minister Sahib Singh on Tuesday said he was removed from the Chief Minsiter's post because the Bharatiya Janata Party (BJP) leadership felt that despite his best efforts, some problems remained unresolved.

Talking to reporters at his Shalimar Bagh residence, Mr. Singh said: "I admit that in some areas, the Government could not satisfy popular aspirations during my tenure as Chief Minister. I take full responsibility for whatever grievances were left unresolved. That was the reason why the party decided to replace me with Ms. Sushma Swaraj. The party felt that she was the right person to increase the pace of development. I just hope the new Chief Minister solves the problems which I could not."

Even as he lauded the development works done during his tenure, he dedicated the achievements to the Delhi Cabinet and party workers. "I am proud of the work I did in the last two-and-a-half years. I could have done more if the Assembly had more powers. That is why I had strongly taken up the cause of full statehood to Delhi. Now, as the Union Government is led by the BJP, it should not take much time to redress these problems," Mr. Singh said.

While the former Chief Minister admitted that price rise was one of the issues which affected people. He said onion prices would come down soon, as an order to import 13,000 metric tons had been passed during his tenure.

On law and order, Mr. Singh said the situation was not up to the mark but the Government was helpless as it had no effective control over the subject. However, he said "the Union Home Minister was very keen to improve law and order in the Capital and had planned certain measures. It will take some time before these measures were actually translated into results."

---

* *Pioneer*, New Delhi, dated October 14, 1998.

In an indirect reference to the overwhelming support from the Jat community, he said: "I am thankful for the kind of support which is being extended to me by a particular community after I stepped down from the Chief Minister's post but I want to emphasise that I belong to the whole rural community."

"I noticed that unchecked migration of people from rural areas created problems in the urban centres. The migration also created certain problems in the rural areas. Therefore, I took special interest in development of rural areas to create a situation where better opportunities were provided to people," he added.

After a 'mahapanchayat' in Bawana village on Tuesday, people in the rural areas had decided not to vote for the BJP. Asked how he would convince these people to vote for the party, Mr. Singh said: "I will go there and convice them to vote for the party. I hope they will agree with me."

It is All a Matter of Timing*

With Prime Minister Atal Behari Vajpayee deferring the expansion of the Union Cabinet, the Bharatiya Janata Party is showing signs of decision-making. In light of its allies' instability and the party's internal squabbles, this was indeed the right thing to do. In Delhi, Chief Minister Sahib Singh had to go. It must be remembered that besides the usual crisis of power and water, Mr. Singh's tenure also witnessed the move to ban "skirts" so as to prevent girls from contacting malaria from mosquito bites; a ban on certain religious customs in churches; and, of course, the wise words that onions are a food for the rich! The BJP has moved rather late in the day but it has taken a step in the right direction. Ms. Sushma Swaraj is competent, combative and may well swing the trend in favour of the BJP in the Assembly election next month.

Of course, there are still many hurdles to be crossed. But the Congress has been sitting pretty even as the BJP has blundered on with self-inflicted wounds. The Congress has a great weakness in its President, Ms. Sonia Gandhi, going by the

---

* Pioneer, October 19, 1998.

manner in which the electronic medium projects her. Every time Ms. Gandhi reads out her speech in an alien accent she raises more questions than answers. Cosmetic changes and imitating Indira Gandhi's style of walking are fine, but in an age of constant media attention the negatives are difficult to camouflage. The BJP has refrained from personal attacks, which is the correct thing to do. The Congress may suffer from dynastic tunes but the voting public might have different ideas. The BJP has a rather difficult task ahead but the fact that it has taken stock of the situation in time and decided to put its best foot forward is a positive sign.

Mr Sahib Singh's supporters "gheraoed" the BJP president the moment the former was replaced. What better proof does the BJP need of their capability? Rights and wrongs are seldom easy to define but Mr. Sahib Singh, in the public perception, is responsible for the horrific law and order situation in Delhi, the dropsy epidemic and the weak response to the crisis, the worst water and electricity crisis faced by the Capital in recent times, apart from a huge hike in school fee and every other imaginable catastrophe.

However, the BJP has taken the right decision at the wrong time. The reality is that this change should have been effected at the time of the Lok Sabha elections earlier this year. If the BJP had done it then, it would have swept the polls. But this did not happen as the BJP's decision-making at the top was vertically split between Mr. Atal Behari Vajpayee and Mr. L.K. Advani. The situation is hardly any different today. The chaos surrounding ticket selection, divided into two warring camps, can certainly create additional problems.

As far as Delhi is concerned, the current decision has been simmering for over six months now and out of ten senior BJP leaders, eight admitted that Mr. Sahib Singh was an absolute disaster as a Chief Minister. The BJP had several alternatives—Madan Lal Khurana, Jagmohan, Sushma Swaraj, Vijay Kumar Malhotra. Mr Advani, along with the RSS, stood by Mr. Sahib Singh while many others were happy to see the effective Madan Lal Khurana sidelined.

Mr. Vajpayee, consistent with his stance on most subjects, continued in a detached manner and things simply went from bad to worse. Mr. Advani identified with the coming disaster and persuaded the RSS to effect changes and Mr. Madan Lal Khurana was given the green signal on October 9. The green signal however turned red when Mr. Sahib Singh used his clout and Ms. Sushma Swaraj emerged as the compromise candidate. Mr. Khurana and the Punjabi lobby was duly ejected and everyone claimed that all was well and even the price of onions showed a perceptible decline!

The Delhi episode shows that the BJP's problems are only beginning and now, besides Mr. Madan Lal Khurana and Mr. Sahib Singh, there will be a third force to reckon with in the form of Ms. Sushma Swaraj. Prime Minister Vajpayee has his own set of problems because the "J" bomb continues to tick, a reason why I am not surprised that the Cabinet expansion was deferred. AIADMK supremo Jayalalitha simply cannot be ignored and her allies who had deserted her will have to wait "indefinitely" for their respective portfolios. The internal bickerings in the Tohra-Badal camp in the Shiromani Akali Dal are apparent. The Udham Singh Nagar issue has few solutions; the three member committee is only there to gain time as Mr. G.S. Tohra has already said there is nothing to discuss. The Punjab supremo has also asked the BJP not to induct his nominee, Mr. Chandumajra, till the issue is resolved. Mr. Prakash Singh Badal's nominee, Mr. Dhindsa has been rejected for the post of Governor of Rajasthan and there is general chaos in Akali politics. The contradictions in the Bihar Samata Party and the BJP in Orissa are equally complex and there are few solutions in a situation where every one wants to be a minister.

The BJP hopefuls are no less demanding and, simply put, every MP wants to be a minister. Foreign visits, particularly to the United Nations, to project the Indian viewpoint on a variety of issues are little compensation but provide temporary relief to a chaotic coalition. I feel that Prime Minister Vajpayee has taken the right decision. The cabinet expansion will not come till after the Assembly elections and will be further deferred if the results are not favourable.

The reality of politics is that every leader has several attachments. The power syndrome requires many an "operator" and every individual also has his personal agenda. Internal wars to secure the leaders' attention and the desire for a piece of the "cake" cuts across ideology and belief. Internal power game has many winners and losers and in the forthcoming Assembly elections in Delhi one will first witness intense internal battles between the followers of Mr Vajpayee, Mr. Advani and the RSS man, Mr. Sudershan. The Congress party's internal wars will rage between Messrs. Arjun Singh, Natwar Singh, Shiela Dixit and Vincent George as candidates approach different lobbies for tickets. The battle for the people's votes will only start after the internal power struggles in both parties have drawn blood. There is nothing unusual in all this as the power game relentlessly moves on and in a fluid state especially the warfare tends to become rather intense.

Political beings will realise that divisions in society and increased lawlessness will only make governance close to impossible and vested interests with very long arms, with many linked to criminal mafias, will control events in the coming future. Many will be silenced as few like to take up cudgels, and the "haves", who have much to protect, rarely dare the elements. Change and progress comes with commitment and a thought for the future. Change will perhaps come with a complete revamp of the system. Unfortunately, however, change will come only when we are at the brink of disaster. Even as battlelines are being drawn for the future, we wait for the system to be ripped apart.

Campaigns may Decide Poll Results*

With the Prime Minister, Mr. Atal Behari Vajpayee, pitted against the Congress president, Mrs. Sonia Gandhi, Delhi is set to witness some high-voltage electioneering as the race for power in next month's assembly elections hots up.

The electorate is yet to give a clear indication of its inclinations, and the main rivals—the ruling Bharatiya Janata Party and the Congress—as well as the smaller outfits—Bahujan Samaj Party and Rashtriya Loktantirk Morcha—are chalking out an ambitious campaign programme.

---

* Statesman News Service, New Delhi, 20.10.98.

Leading the pack are Mr. Vajpayee, who will set the ball rolling for the ruling Bharatiya Janata Party at a rally on 24 October, and Mrs. Sonia Gandhi, whose campaign schedule is being chalked out by the Congress. She is expected to address a series of meetings virtually covering the entire city.

The Rashtriya Loktantrik Morcha leaders, Mr. Laloo Prasad Yadav and Mr. Mulayam Singh Yadav, are also scheduled to address a public meeting to gauge the mood of voters and mobilise their supporters.

And the day Mr. Vajpayee addresses the BJP rally—at Chattrasal Stadium in north Delhi—the BSP leaders, Mr. Kanshi Ram and Ms. Mayawati would be engaging in a show of strength at Ramlila Maidan.

Incidentally, Ramlila Madian was the original choice for the venue of the BJP rally, but the party had to settle for Chattrasal Stadium as the ground was already booked.

It is expected that the Congress and BJP would be going all out as there was no clear indication about the mood of the electorate yet.

Random surveys have shown that voters are not entirely satisfied with the BJP's performance in Delhi but are yet to come out in complete support of Congress.

In such a situation, it would be the nature and thrust of the campaign by rival parties which might clinch the issue.

The Congress has already organised scores of meetings and dharnas to protest the BJP's "failures" but it is banking heavily on Mrs. Sonia Gandhi to clinch the issue. Other senior Congress leaders are also expected to chip in after Mrs. Gandhi moves on to other states.

She had addressed a well-attended rally near Mandi House two months ago and the party is hoping to receive a similar response once Mrs. Gandhi hits the campaign trail in Delhi.

The BJP has been concentrating on revitalising its organisation and its leaders claim everything is now in place for a bid to retain power.

It has organised conventions for linguistic groups and its youth wing held a scooter rally last week. Their leaders are now concentrating on making the Chattrasal Stadium rally a grand success.

Dikshit Hits Out at BJP for 'Political Gimmickry'*

Delhi Pradesh Congress president Sheila Dikshit on Wednesday said that the move by the Prime Minister to induct Sahib Singh, into the Cabinet "through a letter of his intent was nothing but a political gimmick". In a press statement, Ms. Dikshit said, "It is unprecedented in the history of Cabinet formation in India that an offer is made by the Prime Minister through a letter of his intent to induct a colleague into the cabinet. This is a mockery of a system's sanctity, wherein such communications are addressed to the President of India."

"The latest in the series of damage control exercises by the BJP, wherein Sahib Singh was offered a berth but he refused, cannot fool anybody and people can see through this political gimmick", the statement said.

The DPCC chief said, "instead of attending to the problems of the people regarding price rise, scarcity of electricity and water and falling law and order problem, the BJP is again indulging into the political tricks."

"The tears that followed from the refusal of Sahib Singh to join the cabinet is perplexing. I wish the tears could have also been shed when the people were suffering from water and power crisis in the summer and not able to purchase vegetables and onions because of price rise", she said.

Atal Launches Poll Campaign—PM Promises Full Statehood to Capital**

Prime Minister Atal Behari Vajpayee today launched the Bharatiya Janata Party's campaign for the forthcoming Assembly elections with the announcement of granting full statehood to Delhi. However, the most persistent campaigner for full statehood, Union Minister Madan Lal Khurana, was conspicuous by his absence.

The public meeting started with Delhi Pradesh BJP president Mange Ram Garg ridiculing the opposition parties' attempts to bring down the BJP government in Delhi. Mr. Garg's

---

* The Hindustan Times, Correspondent, New Delhi, Oct. 24.

** *Pioneer*, New Delhi, October 22.

digs at the Congress leaders were followed by former Chief Minister Sahib Singh Verma's emotional tirade. Mrs. Sushma Swaraj on her part declared that she could "sense victory" and that partymen would together "conquer' the Old Secretariat once again.

Others present at the function included senior leaders Vijay Kumar Malhotra, BJP spokespersons Venkaiah Naidu and K.L. Sharma and Chandni Chowk MP Vijay Goel, East Delhi MP Lal Bihari Tewari, all Delhi ministers, MLAs and councilors.

Maintaining that he did not doubt the party's victory in the polls. Mr. Vajpayee said the people had not forgotten that the BJP had inherited a crippled regime and all immediate problems had old roots. He said the BJP had promised full statehood to Delhi and the promise would be fulfilled by the next Parliament session.

"I have always maintained that the way to New Delhi is through Old Delhi. If we can set things right in Delhi, the story will be repeated in the rest of the country. Forming a government in Delhi was part of the solution, giving statehood would be the next step. Simultaneously, we will be according statehood to other declared regions as well," Mr. Vajpayee said.

Regarding the power and water crisis, price rise and onion prices, Mr. Vajpayee said people would have to analyse these issues more realistically and with a wholistic approach. "We had a lot of problems regarding power and water supply this summer. Every big city in the country was facing power shortage. This is the outcome of the previous governments' inability to generate power. Within six months of coming to power, we have decided to set up three big power generation plants which will solve the power problem for not only Delhi but most other parts of the country as well."

Mr. Vajpayee said the year had been marked by floods and landslides due to which crops had been destroyed. The rise in onion prices was due to the destruction of onion crops near Nasik.

"We could not have predicted and prevented such natural calamities. We had even started exporting onion by the time we realised that the crop had been destroyed. We would have purchased onions had we known about the bad weather.

We can only ensure that this does not happen again," he added.

Mr. Vajpayee said it was very unfortunate that leaders had walked out of the Education Ministers' conference because the Saraswati Vandana was being recited.

"The same Saraswati Vandana was recited last year but because the BJP was not in power it was alright. But now they have become so panicky that they have started protesting on such issues. Saraswati Vandana incidentally is part of the Vande Mataram. I would like to ask these Left and Congress leaders whether they would want it deleted from the national song," Mr. Vajpayee quipped.

He said that the Delhi Government would have to work harder towards more efficient implementation of the National Capital Region concept.

Sushma's 'Night Vigil' Improper: EC**

Delhi Chief Minister Sushma Swaraj's night visits to police stations with media and the police commissioner in town, are "improper and these must stop," the Election Commission told the Union home ministry on Wednesday.

Viewing the visits as a gimmick and violating the spirit of the model code of conduct on the eve of assembly elections, the Commission took up the matter at a meeting with the Union home secretary B.P. Singh and the home secretaries of the states going to the polls, EC sources said. The meeting chaired by Chief Election Commissioner M.S. Gill has sought prompt corrective action as the election notification is to be issued on Friday.

While the commission has not put down anything in writing, it is believed to have made it clear that it sees no justification for visits by the chief minister with the appropriate authorities (home ministry), rather than the much-publicised visits, which could be seen as an attempt to influence the voter.

** The Times of India News Service, 29.10.98.

Equally important is the point that the Commission debars government officials from touring with ministers as these visits spoil the level-playing field, envisaged by the model code of conduct. The Commission had recently directed the Rajasthan government not to involve ministers in the disbursement of drought relief. The job could well be left to the civil servants.

The "so-called surprise" visits by Ms. Swaraj with police officers and party supporters would, in all probability, "intimidate" the police force in the Capital, affecting its free and fair functioning during the elections, the sources added.

Meanwhile, security arrangements for elections in Delhi, Madhya Pradesh, Rajasthan and Mizoram were discussed at the one-and-a-half-hour meeting. While the state home secretaries were asked to seal their borders, the Commission has directed the Andhra Pradesh, Uttar Pradesh and Haryana governments to seal their borders to ensure that anti-social-elements did not disturb the elections in the four states. If necessary, the governments should also consider invoking Section 144. The Commission also reviewed the strength of security personnel required in the four states to conduct a free and fair poll.

EC Pulls up Sushma*

The Election Commission has pulled up Delhi's Chief Minister Sushma Swaraj for conducting surprise checks at the Capital's police stations in a manner that could bring undue electoral advantage for the Bharatiya Janata Party in the coming Assembly polls.

The Commission has also asked the Union Home-Ministry to take the necessary corrective steps and to see that the Delhi Police functioned professionally.

CM's Concern for Law and Order Irks EC**

The Election Commission has pulled up Delhi Chief Minister Sushma Swaraj for undertaking police supervisory work in a

* *Hindustan Times*, New Delhi, October 28, 1998.

** PTI, *Pioneer*, New Delhi, dated Oct. 29, 1998

"very obvious propagandist manner" in the Capital apparently violative of the model code of conduct in view of the next month's Assembly elections.

It also asked the Union Home Ministry to take this matter up at the "highest level" for necessary corrective action to ensure a level-playing field for elections and professional functioning of the police. The commission, which reviewed the situation in the states going to the polls, sought an immediate and early action, highly placed sources said.

It pointed out to the Home Secretary that under the law Delhi Police is to function professionally under the direction of the Union Ministry of Home Affairs only, the sources added.

Ever since Sushma Swaraj took over as Chief Minister a fortnight ago, she had been conducting surprise checks at police stations even at midnight and pulling up personnel for alleged negligence.

The commission's warning comes two days ahead of its notification for conducting Assembly elections in Delhi.

BJP's Women Cell Takes Lead in Coining Slogans**

For the first time the women's wing of the Bharatiya Janata Party (BJP) has taken a lead in coining catchy slogans to lure voters. The over a dozen-odd slogans appeal more to women safety by recalling the alleged involvement of the then Delhi Congress leaders in the gruesome murder of Naina Sahani.

A special meeting of the women's wing took place recently for preparing the list of slogans. Interestingly, Mr. Subhash Narota hailing from Maharashtra was involved in the slogan framing exercise.

Several of the slogans revolve around the Naina Sahani murder case, one slogan says *tandoor se bol rahi hai Naina, Congress se bach kar rehna* (Naina cautions people against the Congress). Others are similarly worded like *Naina ka khoon ab rang layega, BJP ka hi raaj Dilli pe aayega* (Naina's murder will bring results by returning the BJP rule in Delhi).

Sources said that the women's wing has decided to start their campaign from November 14. Women in groups of 12 to

---

* Arati Bhargava, New Delhi, November 12.

15 will drive in open tempo through the lanes and bylanes of the Assembly constituencies shouting slogans. About three to four Assembly segments will be covered each day. The campaign will begin from Sarojini Nagar.

Not all the slogans relate to Naina Sahani. Others focus on the party. These include: *Mahilaon ka ek hi arman, mahilaon ka badhe samman* (women's only aspiration that their prestige increases), *jan jan ki ek he aawaz, Dilli per raj Karegi Sushma Swaraj* (People unitedly call for Sushma Swaraj to rule Delhi) and *Vande Mataram apna naara hai BJP ka kamal hame pyara hai* (our slogan is Vande matram and we love the BJP's lotus symbol).

Sources, however, stated that there was much discontent among a section of the women's wing.

A case in point is that of Ms. Shashtri, a member of the Lal Bahadur Shashtri family, Ms. Shashtri joined the BJP in early '90s. She had been tipped to get the party ticket from the Saket Assembly constituency. At the last moment her name was struck down from the list.

BJP Moves in Delhi are 'Numbered'*

Politics, they say is a numbers' game. And Delhi BJP leaders seem to have taken this a bit too seriously.

Three weeks after Mr. Sahib Singh was replaced as Chief Minister, his car, his official residence and his cellphone have no takers. All of them are stated to have inauspicious number, which leaders feel, may have led to his exit.

Two-and-a-half years ago, Mr. Sahib Singh had refused to shift into the Chief Minister's official bungalow—33, Shamnath Marg. The house was considered inauspicious as the then occupant Madan Lal Khurana had to quit in unusual circumstances.

Today, some BJP leaders believe the same for Mr. Singh. About 20 days back, when Mr. Singh relinquished office, he returned the two official cars and his mobile phone to the Government. But here were no takers for these things in the Delhi Cabinet. Even if some of them wanted one of the cars,

* Sanjay Singh, *Pioneer*, New Delhi, dated November 4, 1998

they were too scared. The reason — the numbers might have dethroned Singh.

Mr. Singh's cars bore the numbers—1111 and 9999. While 1111 was in his possession as Chief Minister, the 9999 one came to him in his capacity of being chairman of the Delhi Jal Board.

The cars went to Ms. Swaraj when she took over. Though she retained the Jal Board car — 9999, the other one was replaced by a new one with the number 2222.

So where did the car—1111 go? To Industries Minister Harsharan Singh Balli who had been demanding a replacement for his ramshackle Ambassador. But when Mr. Balli saw the number plate, he cringed.

The number was inauspicious, the person who used it previously had just been shunted. And Mr. Balli did not want to share the same fate, sources said. Mr. Balli's driver came up with the idea of fixing another number over the existing plate. So 1111 was covered by a makeshift 41.

This number had proved to be lucky for Mr. Balli, or so he thought as he was not removed from the Ministry even when the new Cabinet was formed by Ms. Swaraj.

The fact that the Chief Minister could not afford to remove him as he was the only Sikh MLA in the BJP made no difference to him.

After using that car with the fake 41 number for some time, Mr. Balli returned Sahib's car and got his old car back.

As a party leader pointed out: "The assumption of fate being linked with numbers is not wrong. Mr. Singh reached greater heights once he got away from these numbers. Overnight, he became a leader with mass base with a Union Cabinet berth waiting for him."

Well, Point Taken and Number Noted!*

Sikh Forum Calls for Boycott of Congress*

Peeved at the Congress decision to bring forth several leaders who are alleged to have played a role in 1984 anti-Sikh riots, the Sikh Forum, a body of prominent Sikhs in Delhi, has called

---

* Staff Reporter, *Times of India*, 10.11.98.

for the boycott of Congress candidates in the forthcoming assembly elections.

A statement released by the Forum on Monday stated the Sikhs in the Capital had supported the BJP in the last elections to keep the Congress out of power. "But the performance of the BJP has also not been upto our expectations and the promises made to us have not been fulfilled so far," the statement said. The statement was issued on behalf of R.S. Narula, Lt. Gen. J.S. Aurora, Jaspal Singh, Amrik Singh, J.S. Neki, Maheep Singh, M.S. Batra, Harbhajan Singh Nishkam. Ajaib Singh, M.S. Phoolka, A.S. Narang, Col. Manohar Singh, Sharanpal Singh, Wg Cdr R.S. Chhatwal and Surinder Singh.

The statement has also called upon the BJP leadership to assure the Sikh community of fulfilling their demands in a time-bound manner. These include disbursement of enhanced compensation as per the high court order to the 1984 riot victims and to ensure decision of disputed cases through a tribunal.

Interestingly, the Forum has also asked the BJP government to exempt Sikh women from wearing helmets while riding two-wheelers.

Vajpayee Goes Cong.-bashing in Delhi*

It was Prime Minister Atal Behari Vajpayee's day with the voters of Delhi today. For Ambedkar Nagar in the morning, Gole Market in the evening, he kept up his attack on the Congress for spreading misinformation in order to return to power.

Vajpayee mesmerised the voters in his inimitable style in a series of rallies across the Capital for the November 25 Assembly election. Most of the leaders of the Delhi BJP were in attendance at these high-security meetings, the major ones being in Khanpur, Kidwai Nagar, Vishwas Nagar and Gole Market.

"Why is there no Congress Government anywhere, except in Madhya Pradesh, Orissa and Mizoram? Because to day the

* *Express News Service*, New Delhi, November 13.

Congress is synonymous with corruption. But they cannot stay away from power too long. So they are desperately hatching conspiracies to defeat the BJP and usurp power," he said.

Vajpayee went on to say that the Prime Minister has been brought under the purview of the Lok Pal Bill much against the wishes of the Congress. "The Bill will be tabled during the Winter session, we'll see whether the Congress supports the Bill," he added.

"It would be better if elections are fought on issues of development. But to win the elections the Congress is indulging in petty politics and unfair methods by which neither the people nor democracy will benefit," he said. Narrating an incident from his childhood in Kanpur, Vajpayee said that the Congress is spreading rumours the way the British rulers in India used to create trouble and to cling to power.

The Prime Minister accused the Congress of pursuing "negative politics" in its bid to grab power and said the trend was not good for a healthy democracy. He said the Congress had been telling the people that there would be communal riots and violence and the country would be divided on the basis of religion, language and culture, but there had been no communal clashes in the past five years of BJP rule in Delhi.

"It is in the Congress ruled Madhya Pradesh that women of a minority community have been sexually assaulted. But the honour of a woman should never be made a political issue. In fact, we are for awarding the death sentence to culprits who assault women's modesty," he said.

The PM described Delhi as a micro-India with people of all states and languages residing here. He also talked about the fact that Delhi's population is increasing at twice the rate of the rest of the country which was creating pressure on Delhi's amenities, housing, universities and roads.

Among the national leaders who shared the platform with him were CM Sushma Swaraj, ex-chief minister Sahib Singh Verma, Maharashtra Deputy CM Gopinath Munde, Himachal Pradesh Ex-CM Shanta Kumar and ex-governor of J&K Jagmohan.

Sushma Swaraj will Win, but will the BJP?*

Her worst fear could be turning out to be true. BJP chief minister-designate Sushma Swaraj is all set to win against a little-known Kiran Walia of the Congress from Hauz Khas. But her party, if a couple of pre-poll surveys (including one by CMS) are to be taken seriously, is inching towards a major defeat.

Perhaps nobody knew it better than Sushma herself when she took over as Delhi Chief Minister less than two months ago. She had categorically expressed her reluctance to give up her union ministership to become Delhi CM. And the cause of her reluctance is now becoming more apparent with each passing day.

But, as she had said then, "as a loyal soldier" she had no option but to take up the responsibility. It is because she did not want to burn her candle at both ends that she did not resign from her MP seat. (An MP is entitled to keep the seat for six months, even while taking up another political job.)

The Congress has already exploited this by saying that she has been committing a 'fraud' on people by keeping her career alive through her MP seat.

It has made things worse for Sushma. If she chooses to retain her MP status, there will be no formidable leaders with mass base left to lead the local BJP. Sahib Singh has already been assured a berth in the Union Cabinet and he loses no opportunity to score the point that he is waiting for the Prime Minister to invite him to take an oath as Cabinet minister. Madan Lal Khurana too is with the Centre.

On the second rung of the BJP leadership in the Delhi Assembly, the only people left are Dr. Harsh Vardhan, Poornima Sethi, Jagdish Mukhi, Mewa Ram Arya, Nand Kishore Garg, Rajendra Gupta and Harsharan Singh Balli, who do not have a mass base. In fact, they too will be counted only if they emerge victorious in the elections.

The CMS poll survey indicates the Congress may get 40 seats, while the BJP may finish with 26 seats in the 70-mem-

* Raman Kirpal, *Indian Express*, New Delhi, November 18.

ber Delhi Assembly. The CMS poll, however, said 14 per cent voters surveyed were undecided.

In the past two weeks, the articulate Sushma tried to get the best out of the situation she was put in.

The moment she chose the Hauz Khas constituency, she knew she would not have to work too hard for her victory. The Hauz Khas voters, as the electoral results show, have been very kind to the BJP during Parliamentary as well as Assembly elections, even in its worst times.

In the past 10 days, thus, she spent as many as seven visiting the constituencies. She apparently drew up a strategy to sell her "winnable" image to other constituencies by declaring that her victory does not matter if they do not vote for the other BJP candidates.

In one public meeting at Sultanpur, she said: "If the police remain alert, there will be no crime. If the electricity employees are available at the complaint centre, your complaints will immediately be redressed. And if you will send Kulwant Singh Rana (BJP candidate) to the Assembly, Sushma Swaraj will become the CM."

This is the exit line that marks all her rallies. It also provides evidence that she could find herself in a situation where she wins the battle but loses the war.

Sushma, Sheila and Sonia*

Assembly'98, the "onion saga", the mini-referendum, call it what you will. But one could not fail to notice that in the recent elections to the Delhi, Rajasthan, Madhya Pradesh and Mizoram State Assemblies, women were centre-state. This is not because of the stereotypical belief that the price of onions matters more to women than to men as they have to manage the household budget and feed their families. It is because Sushma, Sheila and Sonia have been in front and behind the election results.

The battle for Delhi was a clear fight between Sushma Swaraj and Sheila Dikshit. The editor of one newspaper spoke

---

* Kalpana Sharma, *Hindu*, dated 6.12.98.

of it as the battle of "the hand bags", alluding, I presume, to the symbol (a mice inappropriate in this instance) used to describe the indomitable Mrs. Thatcher. Another magazine described them thus: "One is the haranguing housewife; the other the silks and pearls soignee. One is fighting to keep her job: the other is struggling to get it" and so on.

Why a woman of Ms. Swaraj's obvious competence has been reduced to a "haranguing housewife" stereotype is hard to understand. But worse follows. Typical of the media which chooses to focus on what women politicians wear rather than what they say, or think, or do, the same magazine described Ms. Swaraj in these words: "The sindoor is still there, but it has been toned down from its aggressive overtones to a docile kind of look. The saris vary from dull blues and greys to colourful reds and greens. As for the CM herself, gone is the reluctance with which she took her job. She is enthusiastic about governing Delhi and seems reconciled to a stint at State-level politics." Fortunately, the last sentence tells us that the journalist is writing about a politician; you would have a hard time guessing otherwise.

And of course the ubiquitous Sonia Gandhi was everywhere during this election, on posters and hoardings and in the press as she campaigned. In many ways, the spectacular performance of the Congress(I) in three of the four States could be credited to her shepherding and energising a demoralised party after the last Lok Sabha elections.

While these three women were in the news, the two who have been constantly in the limelight ever since the Bharatiya Janata Party-led coalition came to power at the Centre in March, are once again in the eye of the media—Jayalalitha and Mamta. Ultimately, these two women could decide whether we will face another general election soon or whether the Vajpayee government will survive a while longer.

And interestingly enough, the election campaign brought to our notice that after years of hearing only male politicians speak on behalf of their parties, at least two leading parties have appointed women as their spokespersons. Ambika Soni for the Congress(I) and Jaya Jaitley for the Samata Party.

Where have all these women sprung up from and how come they have reached these prominent positions in their respective parties around the same time? While Sonia, jayalalitha and Mamta are known entities, the rise of Sheila, Sushma, Jaya and Ambika (her re-emergence after many years in the wilderness) is fairly recent. Some will argue that these women have made it because they are close to those who run their parties. But no political party will appoint fools when the stakes are so high. In any case, how do most male politicians rise in party ranks? Surely not on the basis of their calibre alone?

One need not cut too fine a point on this issue but I do wonder whether all the talk and the fight over the last three years for one-third reservation of seats for women in Parliament has begun to have an impact within some political parties. For it is possible that the male-dominated party system has at least partially woken up to the fact that the women's vote matters and that there are capable women politicians in their midst who ought to be used much more effectively.

Sushma Swaraj, for instance, before she was pushed into taking over Mr. Sahib Singh Verma's job as Chief Minister of Delhi, was a most effective spokesperson for the BJP. Even those who dislike the party would have to acknowledge that. Similarly, even if the Samata Party's line of reasoning in supporting the BJP is hard to swallow, one has to acknowledge that Jaya Jaitley projects a far more reasonable image of her party than any of its male leaders.

It is also noteworthy that this time, the Congress(I) made a special effort to give more seats to women in the Rajasthan elections. At the time of writing, the detailed results were not available to know how many of these women actually got elected. But as a result of this decision, women's groups in Rajasthan actively campaigned for some of these women candidates and against some BJP candidates who had distinguished themselves in office by their anti-women remarks and actions. Against this background, it is particularly unfortunate that an ostensibly "progressive" party like the Communist Party of India (Marxist) has not yet woken up to the fact that it has to make an effort to encourage women to join it and rise in its ranks. One of its most outspoken and committed women leaders, Brinda Karat, resigned from the central committee recently as a protest against the party's insensitivity to gender. In contrast, the Communist Party of India (CPI) seems to have taken care to keep its women members happy and encouraged them into positions of leadership. Geeta Mukherjee was one of the Parliamentarians who was in the forefront of the campaign for reservation of seats for women in Parliament and remains convinced that this is a step that must be taken. Perhaps she knows only too well the difficulty that women face within Left parties to get into positions of leadership.

But even though women were at the centre of this recent election, they were almost totally absent from the ranks of the political pundits and psephologists who held forth for hours on end on television about the elections. Has the media not produced a single woman who can analyse and comment on political developments to break the monotony of this galaxy of men in suits?

Delhi alone has several senior women journalists who have covered politics for many years and are astute commentators on political developments. How come television could not find a place for Neerja Chowdhury, Seema Mustafa, Neena Vyas or Mrinal Pande, to name just a few? These women would not have been your standard "pretty-face" used to read the news but would have commented shrewdly on the developments taking place. Perhaps they were too busy doing their job to find the time to be on television. But it is striking how often such able women within the media are overlooked when it comes to analysing or commenting on political developments.

Sushma Swaraj: The Face Value*

"My leaders were looking for a universally acceptable face": this is how Mrs. Sushma Swaraj answered the question, "Why have you been chosen to replace Mr. Sahib Singh Verma as Delhi's Chief Minister at this juncture?" The election was knocking at the door. Mr. Madan Lal Khurana could be a good choice if Sahib was to be give the marching orders. . . .

Mrs. Swaraj's "sultanat" proved short-lived for her and distressing for the Bharatiya Janata Party. But most people

---

* Kamaleshwar Sinha.

were convinced by the fact in her reply — her face — her universally acceptable face. After her reluctance to switch on her charm, immensely enhanced by her winsome oratory and wit, she did precisely what her leaders wanted. The face does matter. Travel back in time and meet Christopher Marlowe.

"Was this the face that launched a thousand ships,
And burnt the topless towers of Ilium?

One cannot be facetious about this daughter of Haryana. She took her assignment seriously and won her Assembly seat. Many onion-seekers of Hauz Khas wiped the tears on their faces and voted for her. But they did not vote for her party. Her leaders saw an autumnal face at the onset of winter.

Mrs. Swaraj tends to look at the rout of the BJP in Delhi not quite with her "universally acceptable face". And she has her reasons. She has not been rehabilitated at the Centre. Her Information and Broadcasting Ministry has gone to a less impressive person, Mr. Pramod Mahajan. Her additional charge of Communications has been passed on to Mr. Jagmohan. Both of them are practically Delhiites. The area of statelessness is represented by Mr. Madan Lal Khurana, a Delhi man. Why has the BJP shut its door on her at the Centre? Listen to Prime Minister Atal Behari Vajpayee *"Unhone use me* (in the ministry) *ruchi nahin dikhayi*!" And then read what Mrs. Swaraj has to say: "I met Vajpayeeji this (Saturday) morning and he asked me to quit the Assembly seat." Then make your own judgement.

Chief Minister Sheila Dikshit is happy. So is Dr. Kiran Walia, who was defeated by Mrs. Swaraj in Hauz Khas. But, surely, the former Chief Minister cannot be expectedly jubilant. Her leaders will make her the party's spokesperson or try to mollify her otherwise. But her parliamentary constituency too is in South Delhi. She has been victorious twice. All who know something about her fighting spirit also know that the proverb, "a good face needs no paint", remains true in her case. She has not written off her future.

Battered Swadeshi—BJP Hawks get their Beaks Broken as PM Brooks no Challenge*

DAMN the party and the parivar; lift ideological anchors; full steam ahead with power. The skipper, Prime Minister A.B. Vajpayee, will steer the ship of the state and call the shots, too. No more dual control over the party-government setup.

Doubts about who would be in charge were dispelled at the BJP national executive in Bangalore in January, "While widest consultations (with the party and the parivar) are desirable and necessary," he asserted, "decisions of the government are final."

Party president Kushabhau Thakre had demanded at the behest of the RSS that the government consult the party before taking major decisions. At the end, however, he disappointed the swadeshi lobby saying, "We don't want to be backseat drivers." He even conceded that the government could ignore the manifesto and the national agenda of governance.

It was clear that the party would not sacrifice the government on ideological altar. "Why sacrifice a government for a few slogans," asked a Vajpayee camp follower.

Though temporary, the truce may last till the November assembly elections in Andhra Pradesh, Karnataka, Goa and Sikkim. Until then, party workers will defend what they consider indefensible: why swadeshi is buried, why the patent bill is signed, why foreigners are allowed into insurance . . . .

The RSS had pitted the wrong man against Vajpayee and Finance Minister Yashwant Sinha. Though an RSS pracharak for 56 years, the genial Thakre backed out when chips were down. Surrendering, he said; "The RSS and the BJP are separate. Each takes its own decision."

The New Year resolution apparently is to let Vajpayee rule without any swadeshi or Hindutva hangup. "Because of coalition, certain items we have to leave," said Thakre." . . . There is no question of implementing them."

The swadeshi lobby had insisted that the Hindutva and swadeshi agenda had given the party a distinct identity. But

---

* R. Prasannan, Bangalore, Jan 17, 1999.

those in power prevailed, saying it was desirable to create a new identity as a party of good governance.

Drubbed in recent assembly polls, the party believes that its main task is to win the coming elections. The face-off, thus, was between the ideology lobby and the power lobby.

The resurgence of the Congress was hardly a worry for the ideology lobby. In fact, Thakre said: "If the BJP and the Congress finally emerge as the two main poles, it would definitely stabilise the polity and halt the process of fragmentation."

But the power lobby viewed the rise of the Congress as a threat, and got the political resolution drastically amended. Adopting the 'distinct identity' argument, the resolution agreed that the BJP be projected not as a swadeshi or Hindutva party, but as one imbued with the democratic spirit unlike the dynastic Congress.

The ideology lobby was also dismayed at the government's reliance on bureaucracy. It hated the ideologically bankrupt former bureaucrats in the decision-making circuit.

The power lobby pointed out that the bureaucracy could help it tackle issues like population control and judicial and electoral reforms. As a senior leader said, it was with the help of bureaucratic advisers that the government conducted the nuclear tests and resolved the Cauvery dispute.

The swadeshi lobby bit the dust when the economic resolution listed almost all the recent non-swadeshi achievements. The word 'swadeshi' got relegated to the last paragraph. And the resolution advised the government to consult other parties for a consensus on economic issues!

The leadership was at pains to dissociate the party from the attacks on the minorities. From Bangalore, Gujarat Chief Minister Keshubhai Patel ordered a crack down on the vandals, and Thakre had no quarrel with legitimate conversions.

It was clear at the concluding session that the BJP would no longer allow more than one power centre. Vajpayee has asserted his authority but the question is: can the BJP win an election without RSS help?

We Fumbled in Last Leg, Admits Sushma—'But Future Belongs to us'*

Chief Minister Sushma Swaraj on Thursday admitted that the performance of Bharatiya Janata Party (BJP) government in Delhi had been lacking on several fronts, more so during the run-up to the elections.

Ms. Swaraj said the Government had not fared well particularly in solving water and power crisis, rising prices, dropsy and deteriorating law and order situation.

Addressing the mediapersons at 'Face the Press' programme at the Press Club of India, Ms. Swaraj said the BJP would shortly announce its Chief Ministerial candidates for Madhya Pradesh, Rajasthan and Mizoram, going to poll along with Delhi next month.

Ms. Swaraj, however, tried to drive home the point that "the city Government had faltered only in the last lap". "Delhi Government's performance in last four-and-half years had been very good and people appreciated the work done by the Government. People rewarded the BJP by victories in two parliamentary polls and a municipal election," she said.

"But after the Parliamentary elections which were held six months ago, came a bad summer. People became slightly disillusioned with the BJP Government due to water and power crisis, dropsy deaths, rising prices and deteriorating law and order," she added.

Ms. Swaraj claimed that since law and order was not under the jurisdiction of the Delhi Government and rising prices of commodities like onions was a nationwide phenomenon, "the local Government could not be claimed directly". "But people do not ask reasons from the Government, they demand its solution," she admitted.

She claimed that the onion prices would be checked shortly as the first consignment of 75 tonnes of airlifted-Iranian onions under Open General Licence (OGL) was being off-loaded on Thursday.

Listing the pulse polio programme, establishment of another university, highest labour wages and good financial

* Staff Reporter, *Pioneer*, New Delhi, dated 23.10.98.

management as among the achievements of the Delhi Government, Ms. Swaraj said that she would go to the people with the good work done in the past five years under her predecessors, Madan Lal Khurana and Sahib Singh.

"It is on the basis of these performances I would go before the people to seek vote for the party", she said.

About her involvement with Delhi politics Ms. Swaraj said: "Resigning from the Parliamentary seat is not a Constitutional obligation now but all such speculation would come to a rest once I contest the Assembly elections and assume the post of Chief Minister after the party is elected for a second term."

Admitting that she had been reluctant to accept the Chief Minister's post, Ms. Swaraj said this was mainly because she did not want to replace a colleague. "But now that I have assumed office, you will see no lack of will to govern, people will realise that I am not only a pleasant face but a bold face too. Though my hands are tied due the model code of conduct and I only have a month, I will send a clear signals as to what lies for the future."

"The signal will be reflected through my style of functioning which is very substantial and clearly perceptible," she added.

However, she could not give a satisfactory reply to query that she was an outsider in Delhi and had been imposed from the top, sidelining the grassroots workers and the popular leaders. She said: "In parliamentary democracy political party was more important than the individual, every party had a right to formulate its political strategy and the BJP high command felt that it was better to go to the public with a new face and special personality with new projections for the future".

Ms. Swaraj claimed that the local leaders were consulted and the willingness of candidates to contest under a particular leader was clear when they accepted her their leader knowing that she would be future Chief Minister.

Ms. Swaraj said any allegation of a 'deal' between Mr. Sahib Singh and party high command was baseless. "We should appreciate Mr. Sahib Singh's gesture in the right spirit and not attempt to belittle it," she said.

Asked about the disaffection among the Punjabi and Vaish communities, Ms. Swaraj said the BJP did not function along caste lines.

Special Government Outlets Missing like Onions*

Spiralling onion prices and the price of other vegetables and pulses, and the Government's inability to bring them under control has left Delhi citizens angry.

With assembly elections less than month away, the onion issue is sure to make BJP cry.

The Government had claimed that from Wednesday onwards, every person would be given 2 kg onion a week on his ration card through 70 special outlets.

However, a bulk of the people this reporter met said they could find no outlet in their area. Attempts by this reporter to locate such an outlet in South Delhi also failed.

Madan Lal, a resident of Malviya Nagar said, "I do not know of any Government outlet providing 2 kg of onions. It is extremely difficult to even get one kg of onions from the Mother Dairy, what with long queues and vanishing stocks to cope with."

Residents of resettlement colonies, such as Sangam Vihar and Dakshin Puri seem to be worse off. Hawa Singh, a resident of Dakshin Puri says, "Neither do we have a Mother Dairy vegetable outlet, nor did any onion van visit our area. It has been months since my family last got to taste onions," he added. Sohan Lal a resident of Sangam Vihar said, "The Government gives second rate treatment to the residents of resettlement colonies. Government colonies and posh colonies were frequently visited by the Governments onion vans, while our area was never visited." "With vegetable prices and the prices of other food commodities sky-rocketing, how is the poor man going to survive?" he asked indignantly.

Voicing another common concern of Delhiites, Vir Singh a resident of Chirag Dilli said, "Are we expected to go to work, or stand in the long queue to get onions at Safal

---

* Lalit Lobo, *Pioneer*, New Delhi, dated 29.10.98.

outlets?" "It is also not safe to send your wife or children to buy onions from the Safal outlets, because of the near stampede that sometimes takes place, with people making an all out effort to obtain onions," he added.

When this reporter visited the Mother Dairy vegetable outlet at IIT Gate at about 3 pm on Wednesday, it wore a deserted look. The outlet incharge Suresh said, "A small quantity of onions had arrived, which got sold within a matter of minutes." He too was ignorant about any outlets of the Delhi Government providing 2 kg of onions, in the area.

A number of people this reporter spoke to, held the view that Safal outlet and Super Bazar employees were selling a large portion of onion supplies in the black market. Ghansham Das, a resident of Kidwai Nagar said, "The employees of the Safal outlet in East Kidwai Nagar and the Super Bazar at INA market usually claim that onions are sold out within half an hour of starting distribution to the public." "However if one comes later and is willing to shell out Rs. 40 for a kilo, onions will always be made available to you," he claimed. Onions are sold at Rs. 15 per kg at Mother Dairy outlets and Rs. 10 per kg at Super Bazar. Officials of the Super Bazar at INA refused to speak to this reporter.

Sushma Spurns Party Post Offer*

The former Chief Minister of Delhi, Mrs. Sushma Swaraj, has reportedly spurned an offer for an organisational post in favour of a ministerial berth during the proposed Cabinet expansion.

Sources claimed that Mrs. Swaraj was asked to join as one of the vice-presidents of the party and carry on with organisational work. She reportedly rejected the offer and sought her inclusion in the ministry. A party functionary claimed that Mrs. Swaraj and her camp continued to mount pressure on the government to take her back in the Union Cabinet and "if possible return the Information and Broadcasting Ministry to her".

---

* *Statesman News Service*, New Delhi, January 13.

Even though the Prime Minister, Mr. Atal Behari Vajpayee, has not taken any decision in this regard, a large section of the party is opposed to the move. This particular section is of the opinion that "since things are still not cleared about her alleged links with Romesh Sharma, it would not be prudent to pave way for her return to the ministry."

Inspite of her repeated denials of alleged links with the Dawood man, Romesh Sharma, the latter allegedly admitted during interrogation that he knew Mrs. Swaraj.

It was also claimed that following the debacle of the party in the Delhi Assembly elections, her return to the Cabinet would be sending wrong signals. The party was also upset with her for the remarks that "it was BJP which defeated BJP in Delhi".

It was learnt that the party and the BJP leaders have given Mr. Vajpayee a free hand to decide on the Cabinet. It was claimed that even though decision would be taken in consultation with the Home Minister, Mr. L.K. Advani, and the BJP president, Mr. Kushabhau Thakre, the final word would be that of the Prime Minister.

A senior party functionary claimed that in spite of reports of differences between Mr. Vajpayee and Mr. Advani, there was "no question of the leaders parting ways or opposing each other openly". The functionary claimed that even though there were severe differences between Mr. Vajpayee and Mr. Advani over the economic policies, at the end they would stand by each other.

He claimed that this was the reason why Mr. Advani made the hardliners toe the Vajpayee line on the controversial Patents and IRA Bills.

Moreover, Mr. Advani was also using his influence to neutralise the annoyance of the RSS and other members of the Sangh Parivar, including Swadeshi Jagran Manch, against the economic policies of the government.

EDITORIALS

A Desperate Move*

Changing Chief Ministers before an election is considerably worse than changing horses midstream. Neither the horses nor the riders would escape drowning. The BJP leadership may have come to the conclusion that this is the prospect that lay ahead of the party in the Assembly elections which are just six weeks away. In terms of performance, Mr. Sahib Singh Verma should have been dismissed any time in the past five months. Never was a government so distinguished itself with failures on all fronts—pricės, law and order, power and water supply and maintenance of civic amenities—as that of Mr. Sahib Singh Verma in all its months in office. It is a measure of the desperation of the ruling party that it would risk incurring the displeasure of an incumbent Chief Minister on the eve of an election rather than let him lead the party to the expected rout that lies ahead. In the process, it may have done injustice to a lot of people not the least of them being Ms. Sushma Swaraj who is about to be sworn in as Delhi's first woman Chief Minister. Being an outsider to the local politics of Delhi and also someone not well-versed in the organisational affairs of the party, Mrs. Swaraj will find it hard to hold the Delhi unit of the BJP together with fictional squabbles expected to reach the highest pitch when the party elects its candidates for the various Assembly constituencies.

Some kind of logic is discernible in the change only if it is presumed that the BJP has written off Delhi in the

---

* *The Hindustan Times*, dated 12.10.98.

November polls. The party leadership will be right in assuming that its prospects would be none too bright if Mr. Sahib Singh Verma were to be leading it before and at the time of elections. It would have been understandable if Mr. Madan Lal Khurana, the party's leader with the largest following and longest organisational stint, to take over the mantle. Having decided to displease Mr. Verma, the party should have gone all the way rather than look for a compromise choice which would neither please Mr. Verma nor Mr. Khurana nor, in the end, Mrs. Swaraj herself. The timing of the decision, coming as it does at the end of a coordination committee meeting of the ruling coalition, would revive speculation on the much-postponed Cabinet expansion. Mrs. Swaraj's displacement provides two vacant Cabinet posts for defeated BJP stalwarts like Mr. Jaswant Singh and Mr. Pramod Mahajan waiting in the wings after taking the Rajya Sabha route to Parliament, the Prime Minister is in dire need of vacant ministerial slots. Of course, the expectation that Mrs. Swaraj's image of a staid middle-class housewife standing for family values would pay electoral dividends is not wholly unwarranted. The new Chief Minister needs a lot of luck and goodwill from Delhi's citizens and she deserves both. As for the BJP, it has lived up to its reputation of creating a mess in every decision it takes and start thinking later, if at all.

Change in Delhi*

On paper at least, it appears unlikely that the Bharatiya Janata Party's move replacing Mr. Sahib Singh Verma as the Chief Minister of Delhi will set the Yamuna on fire. Many harassed citizens of the national capital may well think—and not entirely without reason—that the installation of Ms. Sushma Swaraj in his place, marks merely a cosmetic change. In fact, the move is so transparent that in no way can it allay the public impression that it has been made only with an eye to the next month's Assembly elections in the Capital. Hence, the ordinary citizen may tend to attribute it to the gimmickry in which political parties often indulge in with the hope of

* *The Pioneer*, 13.10.98.

improving their electoral fortunes. They may wonder, how can the BJP, by merely changing its guard must on the eve of the elections, hope to absolve itself of its administrative failures in the past for which Mr. Verma alone has been sought to be punished. They may be haunted by many more such pertinent questions about the unpredictable behaviour of political parties when they go to the polling booths on November 25.

Thus, it is clear to almost everyone that the BJP leadership has taken a calculated risk in Delhi. The party has had its own compulsions to opt for a gamble. On the one hand, it had to contend with the anger and anguish of the ordinary citizen over the disruption in the supply of basic services and essential commodities. The Delhi unit of the party, on the other hand, is virtually divided into two camps owing allegiance to Mr. Verma and his predecessor, the Union Minister for Tourism and Parliamentary Affairs, Mr. Madan Lal Khurana, respectively. The leadership, therefore, had to per force look for a neutral Chief Minister to avoid exposing the party to the danger of sabotage in the elections. Although not entire for his own fault, Mr. Verma became the focus of public fury against the party. Not infrequently, the people in different residential areas of the Capital staged spontaneous late-night demonstrations in protest against continuous power failures. The situation was made worse by the sudden scarcity and and sky-rocketing increase in the prices of essential commodities. The unprecedented hike in the prices of onions, in particular, showed the local administration's failure to comprehend the problem in good time. In fairness to Mr. Verma, however, it needs to be said that he started personally receiving complaints about power failures. But that neither solved the people's problems nor prevented his removal from the office.

Although this may appear ironical, a factor that will not determine the BJP's success in the elections is the extent to which Ms. Swaraj is able to enlist the cooperation of Mr. Khurana and Mr. Verma. Despite her two victories in the South Delhi Parliamentary Constituency, she is not as familiar with the nitty-gritty of politics in Delhi as her two predecessors. Her job may be made somewhat easier if Mr. Verma is mollified and given some respectable position. However, her problems will not end with this. She has another difficult job of toning up the local administration and making it more responsive. This is easier said than done in view of the model code of conduct endorsed by the Election Commission.

Lady and the Lad—Sahib Singh Sobs; Jayalalitha Plots*

The charade played by Atal Behari Vajpayee, extending a written invitation to Sahib Singh Verma, to join the Union Council of Ministers and the latter taking a rain-check to cash in after the November 25 elections to four state Assemblies are over, is so jejune that it evokes only derisive laughter. The de jure Prime Minister, dare not tamper with his Cabinet without the concurrence of Jayalalitha, the de facto PM, who has put an embargo on any change until some of her unreasonable demands are met. Verma would have grabbed the opportunity to join the Cabinet if only the BJP were in a position to accommodate him. If the results of the Assembly elections go against the BJP, the Vajpayee Government may not be there but Jayalalitha will be, under a Congress dispensation. Verma, who is not a member of either House of Parliament, will be left high and dry.

The BJP has only itself to blame for this sorry plight. During the recent coordination committee meeting of its allies, it was Jayalalitha who was at the centre flanked by Mr. Vajpayee and Mr. L.K. Advani on either side — for the entire nation to see. But for her non-cooperation, Vajpayee would have inducted Pramod Mahajan and Jaswant Singh into his Cabinet long ago. If he divests Vazhapadi K. Ramamurthi of the extremely attractive Petroleum portfolio, a Jayalalitha's demand, S. Ramdoss, leader of the Pattali Makkal Katchi, is threatening to withdraw Ezil Malai, his lone representative in the Union Council of Ministers. What sin has Mr. Ramamurthi committed to deserve this? He stated in public recently that even if the AIADMK pulls out of the BJP-led coalition, he would continue to remain a loyal supporter of the Vajpayee government. Mr. Vaiko, leader of the Marumalarchi Dravida

---

* *Statesman*, 24.10.98.

Kazhagam, a constituent of the ruling coalition, could not get his nominee, Chenchi Ramachandran, inducted as Union Minister of State for Home, because Jayalalitha threatens to expose his proximity to Velupillai Prabhakaran, the LTTE supremo, whom he had sheltered on many occasions. Like the Bourbons, the Sangh Parivar has learnt nothing and forgotten nothing. The more Jayalalitha tries to humiliate and embarrass the BJP, the higher the pedestal to which they raise her. Her sheer opportunism in negotiating with the Congress for a future alliance while remaining a pat of the ruling coalition and Sonia Gandhi's response should have alerted the BJP. In Tamil Nadu, Jayalalitha is getting increasingly isolated. The Tamizhaga Rajiv Congress, MDMK and the PMK, allies of the AIADMK, have drifted away from the Puratchi Thalaivi. In a similar situation in 1996, P.V. Narasimha Rao refused to see the writing on the wall and came a cropper. Vajpayee seems determined to go the way of Rao.

States of Confusion—Whom and What will They Vote for?*

It is a truly befuddling situation for the voters in the four states going to Assembly polls in November. Not because they do not have a clear choice. In Delhi, Rajasthan and Madhya Pradesh, the choice is clearly between the Bharatiya Janata Party and the Congress. But, the choice ends there. The people are being denied more specific options on two counts in particular. They are not being asked, in the first place, to choose between alternative leaderships. Nor is the electorate being told whether its verdict is being sought on the sate issues alone or the Centre's performance as well. Neither of the contenders has tried unduly hard to conceal its confusion on the question involved. Like the BJP's on the leadership issue, conspicuous by contrast with its line in the Lok Sabha polls. The party then went to the people with the slogan of "stable government and able leadership". It also taunted the other parties and their fronts as leaderless. Officially, of course, it has announced the names of its chief ministerial candidates

* *Indian Express*, 29.10.98.

the Delhi Government controls the law and order machinery, the task in reality is discharged by North Block. This dichotomy puts the Delhi Chief Minister in an unenviable situation. In Ms. Swaraj's case, there is another problem as well. She remains an MP while being the Chief Minister and under the relevant law she is permitted this luxury of a dual role for 14 days after she gets elected to the State Assembly. Should she sit helplessly at home for fear of inviting the Commission's ire in case a situation arises forcing her voters in the Parliamentary constituency to seek her assistance for dealing with the police? If the Commission's purpose is just to caution Ms. Swaraj lest she exceeds her genuine role with the sole motive of influencing electoral behaviour, it is possible to share its concern. But if Nirvachan Sadan goes beyond that, it would only further complicate the task of governing the national Capital.

Capital Punishment—The Assembly hasn't served Delhi Well*

The politics of country-made revolvers has reached Delhi. And no matter how loud the protests of party spokesmen, or justifiable their argument that one election-related murder does not make Delhi a murderous capital, the killing of Ved Singh has a powerful symbolic impact that will worsen the BJP's already dim prospects in Delhi Assembly elections. And it is not as if the party's leaders are helping matters. The most public feud between the two former Chief Ministers, Madan Lal Khurana and Sahib Singh Verma, has added a new twist to the murder. Senior leaders like L.K. Advani have made promises but the present Chief Minister Sushma Swaraj, seems to have nothing to say. The Prime Minister may think he is above all this sordid business and, therefore, needn't intervene but he is wrong. The blood spilled at Nangloi Jat tends to add to accusations of his feeble stewardship of the administration.

Starting with Vajpayee, BJP leaders must ask themselves some straight and hard questions. For example, how does it

---

* *The Statesman*, Nov. 15, 1998.

come to pass that a party not very long ago admired for relative discipline can act in so amateurish a manner. One answer is that power has corrupted the BJP far too soon—it has ruled Delhi for only five years and the Centre for less than a year. In all too short a time they have acquired virtually all the trappings of dirty politics. This means one of two things, or both. First, that the party's ideological armour supposed to keep cadres in line is actually a veneer, good for breaking down masjids but too thin to survive the grind of governance. Second, that ideology, no matter how strong its foundations, is a handicap while running governments in that the faithful are offered no guide in sharing the polls of office. Proof of the second comes from the three Chief Ministers the BJP had to install in Delhi over five years, the last appointment barely weeks before the Assembly elections. Every party has its share of ambitions and conspiracies. But the cleverer ones devise a system of carrot and stick to project an image, if not substance, of continuity. Indira Gandhi was a past master at the game, even while she ruthlessly divided to rule. The Communists have their own strategies. The BJP seems to house too many straps and recent experience of letting bureaucrats loose to abuse power as they see fit and the political leadership from the Prime Minister tolerant of the abuses suggests that the party has no strong leader, which is not entirely true. The murder at Nangloi Jat is a reminder nevertheless that the party needs a strong central leadership and that playing the fool from the prime minister's office must stop.

Another question, arguably a more fundamental one is over the system of governance for Delhi. As a recent contribution in these pages showed, the various forms of administration devised for the spatial have never satisfactorily resolved the tension between Delhi as a capital city and a region. Lines of accountability are blurred—following the murder the Union Home Minister was more in focus than the Delhi administration. While there is some case for popular representation, it can be argued that Delhites will be served better without an Assembly but with directly elected executives under Central supervision in the Home Ministry. This is not a perfect system but it will avoid the multiplicity of authorities. Delhites, one suspects, have had their fill of "full democracy".

Belated Honour*

Other than the systematic politicisation of the country's highest civilian award there can be no reason why the award of Bharat Ratna to Jayaprakash Narayan should come almost two decades after his death. Perhaps the right time was when he openly declined any position of power—after the death of Vallabhbhai Patel, JP was widely mentioned as the imminent successor to Jawaharlal Nehru — in the late 1950s. To prove his earnest in this regard, JP joined the Bhoodan movement of Acharya Vinoba Bhave and quit politics. His role as a fiery revolutionary in the freedom movement got washed away by his post-independence drift away from the Congress. Perhaps, the most appropriate time when he should have got Bharat Ratna was the year 1977 when he was the symbol of the county's resistance against Indira Gandhi's Emergency bringing democracy back to the country. The default then was that of Prime Minister Morarji Desai. Over the past two decades, the award of Bharat Ratna to political leaders was more or less motivated by vote bank politics. JP, like Acharya Vinoba Bhave and Mahatma Gandhi before him, did not leave the legacy of even a small vote bank.

It goes to the credit of Prime Minister Vajpayee that he has at long last rectified a historical error, although the steady devaluation of the award has ensured that it is much less of an honour than it would otherwise have been. The process of devaluation has been accentuated by the habit of successive Prime Ministers to announce the nation's highest civilian award at odd times of the year as if the RBI was announcing its credit policy. Almost all the Bharat Ratna awards announced in the past six years came as driblets during the year rather than as solemn honours conferred on a solemn occasion—on the eve of every Republic Day. The state had been reached long ago where even deserved awardees have had to await the decision of unworthy award-givers. The least that can be done now is for governments to revert to the old

---

* *The Hindustan Times*, December 25, 1998.

practice of announcing these awards once a year and establish a tradition as the British have done.

Crime and Citizens*

Union Home Minister L.K. Advani has done well to order the deployment of 11 additional companies of para-military forces in the Capital to assist the beleaguered Delhi Police to maintain law and order. Police Commissioner V.N. Singh, who has been trying hard, with numerically a thoroughly inadequate force, to cope with a crime situation deteriorating rapidly thanks to a combination of social, cultural and economic factors, will doubtless sigh with at least muted relief. The sudden spurt in murders, almost immediately after he released the 1998 crime statistics for Delhi at his annual Press conference on December 21, and particularly the two double murders in Saket, must have been galling to him. The victims in both gruesome instances were old couples virtually leading retired lives. Clearly, a situation in which ordinary citizens live in perpetual dread of criminals is totally unacceptable. They have a right to be safe while walking in public parks or asleep in their houses at night, and to feel that the law-enforcing agencies are doing their job. Unfortunately, in both cases, the criminals have remained untraced so far. Since action has already been taken against three police officers, the effort should now be not to apportion blame but treat the incidents as an eye-openers and concentrate on coming to grips with the worsening crime situation in Delhi.

The Commissioner of Police's laudable interaction with the residents of Saket in the wake of the double tragedy has thrown up several points which merit serious thought. It has shown, for example, that many loopholes in the colony's existing security system can be easily plugged with the cooperation for the residents themselves. For instance, one of the latter has frankly admitted that many of them do not like to share the financial burden of hiring private security guards. Moreover, they would never agree on such a simple matter as how many and which gates of the colony should be kept open

---

* *Pioneer*, dated 29.12.98.

during the night from the security viewpoint. In many cases, it had been found that the people would not part with even basic information about the antecedents of their domestic servants for thorough police verification. There can hardly be two opinions that all these problems—which are common to all colonies of Delhi—will cease only if the citizens exercise elementary vigilance.

There is, therefore, a need for constant interaction between the police and the citizens. Apparently, the "neighbourhood watch" scheme, envisaging such cooperation, is not working satisfactorily. It needs to be implemented with greater vigour. But, the police should also realise that it is not possible for the public to share its burden beyond a reasonable point. It has to bear the ultimate responsibility for maintaining law and order. Nevertheless, the public's cooperation is important and Mr. Singh's direct dialogue with the shaken residents of Saket will no doubt help in restoring the confidence of the people of Delhi.

Act Firmly, Now*

The spate of attacks on churches and missionary schools in Surat and Dangs districts and the outbreak of communal violence in Ahwa town of South Gujarat must be unambiguously condemned by all. These attacks occur within a larger context of a disturbing increase in violence against the minority Christian community all over the country—in Maharashtra, Uttar Pradesh, Orissa, Bihar, Karnataka, Rajasthan and Madhya Pradesh. Such violence, whether in Gujarat or elsewhere, thrives in the climate created by the politics of hate practised by organisations like the Vishwa Hindu Parishad and the Bajrang Dal. It feeds upon their motivated propaganda of an inexortable "dharma yudh" (religious war) that must be fought to curb the "menace" of "forced conversions" by the "enemy".

It is unfortunate that this growing atmosphere of insecurity recently forced the peace-loving Christian community to come out on the streets in an unprecedented countrywide protest. Reportedly, the number of such incidents of violence

---

* *Pioneer*, dated 29.12.98

is larger than the total number of similar incidents since Independence. According to the United Christian Forum for Human Rights (UCFHR) which spearheaded the protest demonstration in the capital, for instance, there have been about 90 attacks on Christian establishments since January 1, 1998; Gujarat alone has counted more than 40 cases in less than six months in 1998. Whether it is the looting of a convent in Baghpat, or the burning of the Bible in Rajkot or the exhumation of a coffin in Gujarat, these incidents attack more than a particular community. They are an attack on a whole way of life. They undermine the pluralistic Indian ethos which has, down the ages and despite the sporadic aberration, allowed space to diverse faiths and cultures to breathe and blossom in the country. They also violate the spirit and letter of the Constitution of India which provides a series of rights to minority communities to safeguard their identities and interests—from Article 25 which gives them the right to profess, practice and propagate their religion to Article 30 which gives them the right to establish and manage their own institutions. As envisaged by the Indian Constitution, democracy is not majoritarianism; it is an inclusive and open system which assures to all minorities safety, opportunities and freedom. Attacks on the Christian community are also likely to have a serious fallout for the Non-Resident Indian community. They may read to the increased vulnerability of the NRI community to intolerant attacks within the countries they have chosen to make their home.

The BJP Government in Gujarat must take immediate steps to dispel the impression that it is at war with itself while the State burns, and that it has remained largely apathetic to the frightening rise of communal violence. It is also necessary for the BJP-led Government at the Centre to unequivocally distance itself from such incidents. Action must not only be taken, but also be seen to be taken, against the instigators of communal violence in any part of the country. Or else propaganda against India, whether carried out by malcontents within or by inimical forces outside the country, may begin to ring true.

The Year of Unreason—From Enriched Nationalism to Fiery Tradition*

A year in the life of a nation is a pause in history. Another formative mark in the calendar of evolution. It provides one more chance to define the paradoxes of the national destiny, to realise the follies of its scriptwriters. That valedictory exclamation *What a year*! carries within it more than the sighs and sorrows of the witness. It is an expression of relief as well: the descending curtain and a new dawn outside the hall of images. So, what a year! With hope and anxiety, we look back. The remains of 1998, as we survey them in the predawn mist of a new millennium, voice the theme of power and paranoia, of ruler demythicised and ruler re-invented. The ground swayed and cracked in Pokharan as the subterranean explosions heralded national assertion. A bomb of enriched nationalism. If Pokharan radioactivated the raw passions of the patriot, the humble onion mobilised the disillusion of the mis-governed. The Prime Minister looked less than poetic, and his prime opponent, the lady in the borrowed clothes of the Dynasty, looked adequately leaderly. And the funeral fire ravaged from churches to movie halls. Still, we won't be writing the obituary in Sanskrit.

It was not in Sanskrit that India endorsed the arrival of the BJP as a party of governance. It arrived in Delhi not in a chariot adorned with comic-book mythology. The triumph of the BJP as the single largest party was the culmination of degeneration elsewhere in the political market. The Congress, like the Liberal Democrats of Japan, was decaying with the memories of power, with the self-repudiation leadership. The Janata Dal, with its social therapy subordinated to personal egos, was falling to the third force of irrelevance. A BJP-led coalition in power marked the right turn in Indian politics. That human face, like a Dubcek from the parivar, was also the most popular face. But there was no romance of the arrival. Those who received the mandate failed to realise its historic resonance. There was no end-of-the-era glow in their eyes, no word of change in their vocabulary. The acts of the

* *Indian Express*, December 31, 1998.

coalition, with India's most popular politician as its manager, ranged from the banal to the bizarre.

The BJP's most significant national statement was singularly bombastic. A nuclear policy based on national assertion and international responsibility exhibited political maturity. The funny thing was that nuclear India could not manage its vegetable markets. Symbols and gestures are not substitutes for good governance. And nationalism is not a one-way ticket to some civilisational Ruritania. In 1998, someone fantasised about the Sanskritisation of the Indian tongue. Tradition and civilization acquired an unfamiliar accent. The culture cop has no place in a nation confident of its own heritage. But we saw the arbiters of culture and morality reducing the idea of India to an idea of paranoia. After all, who was telling us that the end of Indian tradition could begin in the darkness of a movie hall, that Deepa Mehta could start a sexual revolution that would make Indian manhood hopelessly redundant? As the sobering centre of the right remained rather stagnant, the mad periphery continued to invent enemies.

Who were the enemies? Alfred Nobel and other lesser missionaries. True, the enemy is an abiding motif in the mythology of hate. A regulatory diet of 'the enemy' keeps even the Khomeinist with a trishul in a permanent state of vigil. In such a scenario a burning church is a civilisational triumph over the aliens. In India 1998, churches burned to illuminate the politics of hate. The torchbearers of civilization wanted to regain the ancient land. The self-chosen cultural cleanser was the most active personality of the year. In terms of political culture, the technology that activated his mind mocked the technology that activated the bomb in Pokharan. One India kept forward with the immense confidence of a modern nation. It wanted to declare its power and celebrate its scientific talent. It struck a fine balance between power and responsibility. The other India sought out the Great Yesterday, which in the hallucinations of the so-called civilisational man looked so archaic, so ancient, so exclusive.

The Great Yesterday had another manifestation. The Congress party thinks it is India's natural party of governance. In 1998 the party realised that it was not biologically or intellectually capable of managing the future of India. Sonia Gandhi, for long the extra-constitutional Mother India found herself soaring above the dead minds of India's GOP Political necrophilia collaborated with intimations of morality to turn the first widow into the supreme leader. It was the triumph of the dynastic impulse. The year legitimised the inevitability of a Gandhi in the Congress. The term 'end of the Congress century' was quite popular some time ago. Mrs. Gandhi had arrived, and afterlife was a possibility. Perhaps, Sonia Gandhi was not the singular source of the Congress regeneration. The overstretched pause of the BJP leadership also provided life-saving energy to the other party. The result was not so bad: the first note of a bipartisan polity.

Of course, there were moments of pure joy. The batsman dazzled the nation. And the economist received a Nobel Prize. The sportsman and the professor gave moments of pride, and pleasure. So the spectacular was not purely political. There was entertainment too, mostly from the Dravidian vaudeville. Though the silky kitsch from Chennai was not universally entertaining. But the missionary zeal of the Nobel Prize was fantastic.

"India is an ethnographic and historical museum. But it is a living museum, one in which the most modern modernity co-exists with archaicisms that have survived for millennia," wrote a highly impressionistic Octavio Paz. In this museum, exhibits are always jostling for space. We saw their madness, their passion, their power to influence and instigate. We saw the spectacular and the pathetic, the modern and the archaic. The year 1998 only reasserted the magnificence and the madness of that museum. Even in the year of unreason, the Indian who lives outside the make-believe of the reality managers could declare his active autonomy. He refused to be taken for granted. He may not have come out of this year of national redefinitions unscarred. His perseverance has not yet abandoned hope. So our goodbye to 1998 is also a salutation to the Indians who keep the museum as a great idea of survival. What a year! Well, we survived it.

The Enemy Within*

Reports that there were protests, some muffled, some stridently expressed, by senior party members against the incessant interference of the Rashtriya Swayam Sevak Sangh in the work of Central ministries carry an ominous message for the Vajpayee Government. Even as the Prime Minister keeps pussy-footing the Gujarat Government's attitude towards the Christian minority, he must be realising that the real enemy of his Government is neither the Opposition nor tantrum-throwing allies but the BJP's ideological fountainhead—the RSS. Mr. Madan Lal Khurana was among the senior leaders who gave expression to the frustration of BJP ministers in warding off pressures from the front organisations. While other organisations like the Vishwa Hindu Parishad, Bajrang Dal and the Janata Jagran Manch are overt embarrassments to the coalition government at the Centre, the RSS operates behind the scenes, and often below the surface, which makes its influence on the government more insidious than the others. Mr. Vajpayee would not have forgotten that it was precisely this phenomenon—duel membership of the former Jana Sangh partymen in the Janata Party and the RSS — which eventually brought down the Morarji Desai government and led to the break up of the Janata Party. Mr. Vajpayee must remind the RSS that he is running not a BJP government but a coalition and, even if it were a BJP government, its constitutional and democratic obligations would entail keeping the RSS and other organisations as far away from the portals of government as possible. If the BJP wants to expand its popular constituency all over the county it has to break loose from the stranglehold of the RSS.

The purblind acts and attitudes of the BJP front organisations will hurt the BJP most not only by the inevitable shrinking of its mass base but also by scaring away potential allies. The reported moves of Mr. Ramakrishna Hegde to start a new front of parties aligned to the BJP, as of now not to be taken seriously, will eventually lead to a distancing of the allies from the leading party in the Central coalition. In recent

---

* *The Hindustan Times*, January 13, 1999.

weeks Mr. Vajpayee has seemingly obtained a mandate from the party for freedom in making policies and programmes of the Government. But, lacking an ideological alternative to offer to what may be described as the silent majority in the BJP, Mr. Vajpayee's ability as well as willingness to delink the government from the BJP, let alone the RSS, are in great doubt. For a party which aspires to run the national government on its own, the BJP has to become a far larger political entity than be a stifled mouthpiece of militant Hindutva. If there is one person who does represent the moderate face of the BJP, it is Mr. Vajpayee. He has to take the RSS bull by the horn and subdue it.

Still a Captive*

Mr. Atal Behari Vajpayee continues to be a shepherd held captive by his flock. From the day he took over with a statement that he would keep the finance portfolio with him but could not, to the other day when he said at Lucknow that the expansion of his Cabinet would come on Friday, the Prime Minister has simply not been able to do what he wants to do. Time and again, his Government is baulked by the Opposition, the allies and his own party in a manner which hardly does credit to the office or the person. The least that Mr. Vajpayee could have done was to remain silent on the issue until he had finalised the plans to expand the council of ministers to the last detail before making any announcement on it. Prime ministerial announcements even if they were made in passing in the course of informal talks with news persons, should have the imprimatur of an official decision. Obviously the BJP leadership has not drawn the right lessons from the experience of the past nine months in the matter of having broad-based consultations with coalition partners on a regular basis. Whatever victory that the Prime Minister achieved in persuading the BJP to go along with him regarding Government policies and economy-related bills seems to be pyrrhic. Appeasement rather than having one's way seems to be the guiding principle of the Vajpayee dispensation.

* *The Hindustan Times*, January 15, 1999.

The postponement of Cabinet expansion has nothing to do with the ill-conjunction of stars as with the conflicting demands of the allies for not only berths in the ministries but also the portfolios that go with them. Ironically enough, two parties— the Samata Party and the Trinamul Congress—which originally said that they would not join the government but support it as alliance partners are together the cause of Mr. Vajpayee's latest headache. It is believed that Ms. Mamata Banerji wants the railways portfolio for her party and the Samata Party would not like to be deprived of it. In looking at Ms. Jayalalitha as the sole pressure exerciser and possibly, coming to terms with her, Mr. Vajpayee had ignored that there are demanding allies elsewhere. The only way to deal with the situation is for the Prime Minister to tell both his own party leadership and those of the coalition partners that allocation of ministerial berths may be a collective decision but the allocation of portfolios is the prime ministerial right. Unfortunately, Mr. Vajpayee is not insisting on the latter while succumbing to the former. If he cannot satisfy the allies or assert himself, the—only unpalatable choice left to him is to let the whole issue of ministerial expansion be a matter of speculation.